FOREWORD BY CHAP CLARK

# REIMAGINING CHURCH AS FAMILY

RICH GRIFFITH (EDITOR AND AUTHOR) - JJ JONES (EDITOR AND AUTHOR)

SHELLY MELIA - LARRY FOWLER - KEVIN JONES

D6 FAMILY MINISTRY
114 BUSH RD - NASHVILLE, TN 37217 - 800.877.7030 - D6FAMILY.COM

Published by D6 Family Ministry



D6 Family Ministry
114 Bush Road
Nashville, TN 37217
d6family.com

ISBN: 9781614841982
Printed in the United States of America

# WHAT MINISTRY LEADERS ARE SAYING ABOUT THIS BOOK

There is a wind of the Spirit that has brought the need for family ministry to the forefront of church ministry. This book is very much needed and I'm sure will be a valuable resource for church leaders and those studying family ministry. I have such deep respect for all the authors and I'm grateful they included chapters on grandparenting and single parents, which has been missing in some family ministry books. The entire concept of rethinking how we do church as family is spot on. This will be a go to book for our ministry at HomeWord.

—Jim Burns, Ph.D., founder of HomeWord, author of *Doing Life With Your Adult Children: Keep Your Mouth Shut and the Welcome Mat Out*

When a single parent, never married, or blended family walks into church, do they feel at home? It's common for churches to cater toward traditional families (and we certainly want to equip nuclear families), but those with foster kids and different family situations can feel left out. This book has opened my eyes and heart to notice those who aren't happily married with 2.5 kids. Written by a trusted group of experts, this book will help you reimagine church as family—a powerful shift in this lonely age.

—Arlene Pellicane, speaker, author of *Parents Rising*, and host of the *Happy Home* podcast

One of the deepest needs in every human heart is to belong to a family. Part of God's purpose for the church is to be a spiritual family where all are welcome. This book beautifully captures that biblical vision and shows how family ministry is for everyone—single parents, grandparents, foster families, and beyond. This is a timely and needed call to rediscover the church as the family of God.

—Dr. Rob Rienow, Visionary Family Ministries, www.VisionaryFam.com

*Reimagining Church as Family* gives ministry leaders a primer for widening our lens in regard to family ministry. So often our practical strategies cater to the "traditional family" leaving no room for so many others who need a seat at the family table. As a pastor, I am challenged by the work of Rich Griffith and JJ Jones, and I know you will be too. This concise, practical book brings clarity to the sometimes-confusing practice of family ministry.

—Brian Haynes, D.Min., lead pastor of Bay Area Church, author of *War in The Wilderness: Fight for Your Family When Life Isn't as it Should Be* and *The Legacy Path: Discover Intentional Spiritual Parenting*

Through its emphasis on the foundational truth that believers in Christ are a spiritual family, *Reimagining the Church as Family* challenges the church to expand its vision for ministry. The authors powerfully share their insights for including and equipping those who are often overlooked in traditional family ministry, such as grandparents, adoptive parents, and single parents. Wise, heartfelt, and thoughtful, this book inspires us to see new areas where we can be vessels of God's healing and hope.

—Michelle Lee-Barnewall, affiliate professor of New Testament, Biola University and award-winning author of *Surprised by the Parables*

JJ and Rich remind us that *family* is perhaps the most important metaphor the Bible gives us for the Church. And for good reason—

through this lens we see most clearly its beauty, complexity, and yes, dysfunction. Thankfully, having defined the challenges, they bring decades of their own insights, along with carefully curated solutions from practitioners who are actually building *church as family* communities.

—Lloyd Shadrach, co-founding and teaching pastor,
Fellowship Bible Church, Brentwood, Tennessee

My mother-in-law was 19 years old and single when my wife, Karen, was born. Karen did not grow up in a traditional family. But as a young teenager she became a follower of Christ and her local church became the place where she experienced hope, love, affirmation, belonging, and identity. She loved her church family, and they loved her. And that's why I really like this book. It is an inviting call to broaden our thinking and approach to family ministry, anchored in the model of the church as family. *Reimagining the Church as Family* is refreshing and hope-giving!

—Dr. Crawford W. Loritts, Jr., author, speaker, founder,
and president of Beyond our Generation

*Reimagining Church as Family* courageously tackles a crucial truth—family ministry must move beyond traditional models and embrace the diverse realities of those who sit in our pews each week, including single parents who often feel unseen. As someone who has devoted my ministry to championing single adults of all ages and backgrounds, including single parents, I deeply appreciate how this book roots its vision in Scripture, while offering practical and compassionate steps for churches to become a true family of God.

Shelly Melia's chapter on engaging and equipping single-parent families resonates deeply with my belief that the best parent you can be is to be complete in Christ. Single parents deserve a place at the table, not simply as a demographic to be served, but as valuable, gifted members of the church family. This book provides tools and insights to help churches embody the biblical call to love one another as brothers and sisters in Christ (John 13:34–35) and to foster communities where no one walks alone.

I'm grateful to all the contributors for shining a light on the often-overlooked realities of single-parent families and calling churches to reimagine what it truly means to be family. This book is an essential resource for any church leader who desires to reflect Christ's love in the diverse tapestry of today's families.

—Dr. PJ Dunn, founder and minister, Table for One Ministries

Contemporary family ministry presents distinct challenges as well as opportunities for building relationships. This volume discusses how church leaders can foster an environment where family ministry becomes integrated into all aspects of church life, rather than functioning as a separate program. It provides theological perspectives and practical guidance aimed at developing supportive connections within the church community.

—Dr. Ken Baugh, author of *Unhindered Abundance*

# FOREWORD

# A VISION FOR FAMILY MINISTRY

In the late 1990s, 50 pastors from large churches gathered to discuss "Best Practices in Family Ministry." Up to that point, there had been no high-profile, nationwide summit featuring leaders with "family ministry" in their titles. The phrase had been catching on, but by the late '90s, it had become the cutting edge of church ministry.

Since then, while many churches still view family ministry as a vital strategy, there remains no clear, unified definition of what it actually entails—or how deeply it should shape the local church's mission. Traditionally, family ministry has centered on equipping parents and faith communities to disciple children and adolescents. But beyond that core, much work remains.

## A Wider Lens for the Church

This is why *Reimagining Church as Family* is both timely and necessary. Authors Rich Griffith and JJ Jones have invested years researching and practicing family ministry. Along with fellow contributors, they bring the perspective of seasoned practitioners and thoughtful scholars. Together, they guide us toward a broader vision of family ministry—one rooted in Scripture and shaped by compassion.

This book opens the door to seeing the church's mission in new ways. It urges us to move beyond historical stereotypes and to faithfully engage those who may have been left behind, underserved, or overlooked by traditional models.

## A Biblical and Comprehensive Foundation

*Reimagining Church as Family* is a compelling and accessible resource. Though easy to read, it may prompt you to reconsider long-held assumptions and explore deeper truths. From the outset, you'll encounter a biblical theology of family ministry that goes beyond discipling children and empowering parents.

You'll begin to see the church family in broader terms:

- Single-parent households
- Grandparent-led homes
- Families who foster or adopt children
- Even households with all three combined

Most importantly, you'll be reminded of the biblical imperative: family ministry starts with the church as a "family of families" (Ephesians 2:19)—where every person belongs in the household of God, and where we live together as brothers and sisters in Christ (John 1:12).

## An Invitation to Transformation

As you read, take time to reflect deeply on the wisdom and vision offered by the authors. Be willing to be challenged—even shaken. And let us, together as the body of Christ, respond to our calling to be His witnesses (Acts 1:8) to a world longing for reconciliation and redemption.

May the Holy Spirit tear down every wall that keeps us from fully loving others. For every person has been "knit together" by the God of mercy (Psalm 139). Let us welcome, include, and faithfully serve everyone God brings into our path—so they, too, may encounter the beauty of the gospel and the love of Christ.

May the Spirit guide us and use us for His kingdom.

For His sake and His glory. Amen.

Chap Clark, Ph.D.
Executive Director, Institute for Ministry Leadership

# TABLE OF CONTENTS

## Introduction

# A Different Kind of Family Ministry Book

The concept of family ministry is not new. There have been some great legendary advocates and authors for family ministry and if I were to mention some and not others, I would feel horrible for missing some. I (Rich) can tell you individuals who have had a significant impact on my thinking about family ministry. Dr. Ron Hunter of D6 Family Ministry, Mark DeVries, who has written, *Family-Based Youth Ministry*, the many conversations I have had with Dr. JJ Jones and Dr. Chap Clark, who wrote *Adoptive Church*. Not only have I read their books, but I also often use them in my classes as a college professor. Even while I have used other family ministry books, I consider Ron, Mark, and Chap incredible friends as well as influencers. This is important because I know their integrity.

The question comes, "So, what makes this book "different"? In recent years there have been significant cultural shifts in defining *family*. When I was exclusively a youth ministry practitioner, my experience with "family ministry" was limited. What I experienced over a span of time is how family ministry was defined. Family ministry tended to be defined by age and stages of life and, frankly, limited to nuclear (or traditional) families with children in kindergarten through fifth grade. (Throughout this book, we will be using the terms "nuclear family" and" traditional family" as they are synonymous.) I remember having different thoughts about non-traditional families as our youth ministry had a large outreach ministry and these outreach kids could feel left out of our largely traditional family church. Since so many "Family Ministries" were traditional and primarily focused on kindergarten through fifth grade, my next question was, "So, do middle and high schoolers no longer have families?" It was, of course, a hyperbolic and rhetorical question. "What about the students whose parent(s) don't come to church? Where do they fit in?" There was truth in these observations. Age and stage defined family ministry, where parents were actively involved, were often leaving "other ages and stages" out of family ministry. What about grandparents? What about young adults? More importantly, to the point of this book, what about families that are not "nuclear" or traditional families? The more we dove into the issue, under the influence of the mentors listed above, we started to formulate other questions like, "How would it feel to be one of the 'other' families that do not fit in the traditional family role?" and "Why are we only defining family as nuclear (mom, dad, and 2.5 kids) or traditional families?"

Almost a year ago since the time of this writing, JJ and I had a great conversation with Dr. Ron Hunter, Jr. from D6 Family Ministry. The discussion was on families and discipleship. It suddenly hit all of us: "Why are we not defining family theologically rather than just through social constructs? Isn't the theological perspective important?" Truth be told, it was also a genuine heartfelt epiphany for it gave some answers to me, a non-traditional, single dad of three adopted sons. Even as a youth pastor, pastor, and professor, I have often felt like a fifth wheel at church functions. I didn't fit in the "age and stage" model, but I could certainly fit into a theological definition of family! Hear me though, I am a huge proponent of the traditional family. I have had to make up for lacking areas in our family life. However, we must realize that when we constantly shoot only for "the ideal" (traditional families), we leave out a whole lot of families living in "the real" (non-traditional families).

As I work with children, youth, and families at my church where I pastor, and as I work with young adults at the college where I teach, there is one thing I am convinced of: churches need to become family to each other for a number of reasons:

1. Our culture has a huge problem with systemic abandonment (Dr. Chap Clark). For a quick explanation: systemic abandonment is when the institutions and organizations that are supposed to be meeting the needs of our young are hijacked by adult-driven agendas. Chap has written about this, and I have also written how systemic abandonment has led to a crisis in the juvenile justice system. Just a few years ago, the United States had the highest rate of incarcerated juveniles than any other industrialized nation in the world—including Russia and China. (So much for "Land of the free.")
2. Generation Z has been labeled, "the loneliest and most anxious generation." The younger generations have experienced a significant void in meaningful relationships that not only keep them out of trouble but also keep them coming to church.
3. The constant segregation of "age and stage" programming has led to a significant number of young people dropping out of church to never return. They have had a lack of ownership, leadership, mentoring, and multi-generational relationships in the local church.
4. In our culture, there is a significant amount of ephebiphobia (fear of the young) and gerontophobia (fear of the aged) not only in churches, but in our society as a whole. Think about all the news media attention about youth. Most of it tends to be hyperbolic and negative. Here is the

> truth: we fear what we don't know. The reason our young and old might not want to get together is because they do not interact enough with each other and are dissuaded by stereotypes.

I am convinced that the church is the best organization to counter all the challenges I have mentioned above, but that will only happen if we begin to practice not just "church and family," but "church as family"! As someone who has children who were adopted out of brokenness, I can attest to how having a family can make all the difference in the world! Family is a place of joy, growth, challenges, forgiveness, love, and—maybe most importantly—identity and belonging. As children grow and become adolescents, their primary task is identity formation. What better place to belong and form an identity in the family of Christ that we call, "the church"? I am so glad my three sons have always had their local church to call family! The church (and society) misses out when we do not intentionally and frequently bring the young (energy/enthusiasm) together with the aged (experience/insight). As Chap would say (paraphrased), "We need to adopt each other as brothers and sisters in Christ!" I am very blessed because not only did I adopt my sons, but my churches have often adopted us.

We believe that local churches who understand a theological definition of family will become a "church as family" community. In fact, at the time of this writing, there seems to be some research stating that millennials are returning to church post-pandemic.[1] One of the main reasons is that they are seeking community. According to Churchtrac, an organization that shares in some of the Barna research, "Young people are looking for a connection to a faith and a community that will help give them direction while also making

[1] "A New Chapter in Millennial Church Attendance," Barna, accessed April 19, 2025, https://www.barna.com/research/church-attendance-2022/.

a difference in the world."[2] It should be no surprise to any church leader that young people are craving what Jesus gave the disciples: an incarnational, authentic community that helped define them and give them purpose.

Millennials are not the only generation who crave community and belonging. Every person in every generation and all walks of life crave community and belonging. We find this declaration to be true in the Garden of Eden. Adam was in a perfectly good working relationship with God and yet God declared, "It is not good that the man should be alone" (Genesis 2:18, ESV). *Church as family* offers a community of fellowship, belonging, and purpose.

My friend and colleague, Dr. JJ Jones, pastor, co-editor and co-author of this book, has also used the analogy of "adoption" when we "family one another." It is no coincidence that we are thinking this way. First, we both were in the same doctoral cohort with Dr. Chap Clark. Chap wrote two books on the subject. *Adoptive Youth Ministry*, which is a very academic book while *Adoptive Church* is a great practitioner book. I would highly recommend reading *Adoptive Church.* As churches and other organizations make a move toward *church as family*, the Holy Spirit is clearly behind this movement as there are several organizations embracing and training leaders for *intentional* intergenerational ministry.

A few months ago, I (JJ) sat in my department head's office with Tracy and John (not their real names), two singles in our church. We were leading them through a process to launch a new ministry to singles in our church by developing a lay-led team. Tracy and John would become the main lay leaders of this team as they completed this several-month development and training. As we progressed over several weeks, however, the layers of the proverbial onion began to peel away. We discovered that what this particular group desired was

[2] "The State of Church Attendance: Trends and Statistics," Churchtrac, accessed April 19, 2025, https://www.churchtrac.com/articles/the-state-of-church-attendance-trends-and-statistics-2023.

not a new program or an obligatory nod to singles, they just wanted to be seen. To be heard. To have a voice and a place at the table. In a local church that did family ministry very well, we discovered that our singles often felt overlooked, uncared for, and invisible. We championed the traditional family model strongly, but in doing so we often overlooked, not intentionally, other demographics in our church family that did not fit that traditional model. Our singles were not the only ones who felt this way.

Months before this, we began the same process with a group of empty nesters and boomers. Our current "boomers ministry" did successfully launch from this development cohort. But it was birthed from the same desires: to have a place of influence in the local family of faith, to have a voice and place at the table, to be heard and seen. For this group, many in our church were CEOs and entrepreneurs who had started multiple businesses. Now in retirement, they felt that loss of purpose and felt unneeded and unwanted. Many of these church members were key figures who helped start our church 25 years ago. They watched the church grow exponentially as they selflessly gave their time, expertise, and money. They *believed* in the call to start Fellowship Bible Church. Now, many had the question, "Does Fellowship still *believe* in us?" Again, the strong model of family ministry did not have a place to include many who were outside of this traditional family system of a dad, mom, and children.

Our boomer ministry is now a thriving ministry of the church. It is entirely lay led but works with several of our ministry teams. They partner with our young adult ministry to offer "Legacy Nights," in which older adults and young adults share a meal at the table together and have intergenerational exchanges of what it looks like to follow Christ in their life stages. It is a shared learning and ministry experience. Our singles came to the conclusion that their primary desire was simply not to go to our worship service alone. For the average single, especially those who have never been married, it can be quite lonely in a service during child dedications or family Advent readings. We are working with them to develop regular single lunches where friendship can be made, and no one goes to church alone. We must also learn to invite them into the life of the church and rhythms in which the body leads one another, especially on Sundays.

Something else that makes this book different is an implicit understanding throughout of *community*. To be a holistic surrogate family as a local expression of Christ's church, the implication is that we must live in deep communion with Jesus and authentic community together. As Rich has stated, in creation, God desired and designed humankind to be in fellowship with Him and community with one another. In Deuteronomy 6:4–9, God charged His people to remember and practice community principles in their lives with Him, their immediate families, and the community at large. There was no concept of individualism in ancient times; individuals understood themselves to be part of a greater whole, part of a community.

As Rich stated above, we have a burden to see the body of Christ operate as a family, including and inviting all who are adopted in Christ as His children. From the youngest to the oldest, we all have something to contribute for the benefit of the whole family of God. This means we must include those in the family who do not feel a part of the family. And there are more who feel this way than we realize. This is why we have invited the voices we have to contribute to the important project in addition to us. While there are certainly more voices within the family of God we must hear from, we have chosen these as they represent primary, larger populations that struggle with our traditional models.

In the ensuing chapters, I will suggest we need a new way forward, a new way of thinking of family ministry and church holistically. A movement to think of *church as family*, where all ages, demographics, and statuses have a place at the table of family ministry as the extended family of God. To get there I will introduce three pictures and three shifts in our thinking to move us forward. Others will subsequently address how we may engage and equip their chosen population. Their stories will inform and inspire you, the reader.

Shelly will address how to engage and equip single parents. She will lead us to consider three crucial questions as we think about how best to invite single parents and their voice to the table. She will give very practical steps to see, hear, and invite single parents into the life of the church. Larry will address how to engage and equip grandparents as one of the most overlooked and under-resourced people groups in the church. The potential impact of faith formation and legacy that we have (I, too, am a grandparent) as grandparents is more than substantial and, most importantly, biblically encouraged. Rich will address how to equip and encourage foster and adoptive families. No other population has the potential to understand and model our adoption in Christ and what it means for the church to live in community as the family of God than adoptive parents and adopted children. Finally, Kevin will address how to engage and equip perhaps our largest resource in the church, traditional families. As a father, he understands the important role our traditional families have in inviting and welcoming all *kinds* of families to the table as the greater family of God.

As you read this book, ask yourself: Who in your congregation more than anyone needs the church to be a family for them? A young widow or widower with small children? Single parents? The lonely single or divorced person who just wants a place to belong? Senior adults? Grandparents raising their grandkids? The homebound? Special needs? Kids and students from non-churched homes or whose parents are unengaged? In other words, who are the marginalized, the unseen, the forgotten, the lonely in your church? We must think outside the traditional, Western model of family. It is time to see the church through the lens that Jesus and His followers would have seen through their Eastern, communal eyes. Who else needs to be invited to the table, for whom must we set a place? The table is where family sees, hears, and communes with one another. The table of Christ is not just for the ones who model exemplary forms of family or family ministry. Family ministry is not just for the traditional model of family. The table is for everyone. Family ministry is for everyone. This is how Christ designed His Church to function.

## Chapter 1

# Church as Family: A New Way Forward

JJ Jones, D.Min.

What is a family? In our changing cultural landscape, this question is being asked now more than ever. Traditionally, a family is a group of individuals who are connected by blood or marriage, typically sharing a household and supporting one another emotionally, socially, and often financially. For centuries, the family has been defined as a father, mother, and children with extended family living separately. This post-World War II Western ideal of family has become known as the *nuclear* family, an ideal and social expectation that most aspire to attain as they consider the implications of marriage and parenting.

However, in recent years families in America have experienced noticeable changes that have significantly affected the structure of the consummate traditional nuclear family. Noticeable changes such as the effect of divorce, remarriage, interracial marriages, multi-generational households, fostering and adoption, and births outside of marriage have resulted in significant changes in traditional nuclear American families. The rise in divorce rates has caused an increase in single-parent households and blended families. Remarriages have become more common, leading to the emergence of stepfamilies and half-siblings.[1]

Unfortunately, our churches have not kept up. We have, unintentionally, championed a traditional model of family while creating environments that can inadvertently exclude other types of families in the church community. Many of us have heard from various demographics mentioned above, such as grandparents, single-parents, and blended families about how hard it is to connect, belong, and find community. This has never been truer than in family ministry. For many, if you do not fit the mold and model of the traditional nuclear family, you just don't belong. If you have never been married, or have been divorced or remarried, you are less than. Again, this is not on purpose, but it is the implicit message many receive when they visit our churches, especially churches with robust family ministries. When other types of families that are not traditional nuclear families see a lack of intentionally planning ministries that include them, the message they receive is, "We don't matter."

In the same way there are multiple definitions of family, there is also no consensus on just what "family ministry" is, much less how it is best accomplished in the lives of parents in partnership with the local church. The church and the family have traditionally struggled to partner together effectively in the spiritual formation of kids and teens, especially since the inception of professionalized age-graded ministries. The philosophies and models that are currently promoted are as multifaceted and varied as the authors, practitioners, and organizations they represent. Likewise, there can be fragmentation of age-graded ministries in churches, resulting in competition for resources and a siloed mentality among ministries that should be working together and complementing one another. This fragmen-

[1] Alena Demirovic, "The changing face of American families: A 21st century perspective," *Religions,* 18, (April 2024): 18–31. Retrieved from https://www.proquest.com/scholarly-journals/changing-face-american-families-21st-century/docview/3064706969/se-2.

tation was also the result of public education models. Further, the advent of the nuclear family and age-segregation has led family ministry to be defined by age and stages of life rather than a more theological definition of family being comprised of whoever does the will of the Father (Matthew 12:46–50). While we have made very tangible strides forward, many of these models still favor the traditional, biblical nuclear family. And rightly so. Yet, I believe we are still missing an incredible opportunity to minister to the whole of the family of God within our local churches, especially those who feel unseen and unheard.

At the intersection of these current dilemmas, I believe there is a way forward. As stated in the introduction, we need a new paradigm as we attempt to answer this question and move family ministry in the church forward. In fact, what we have discovered is that this is not a new paradigm at all, it is rediscovering a biblical paradigm given to us as adopted brothers and sisters in Christ by Jesus Himself. It is an ancient way, based on the model of how Christ Himself set up His Church to function ... as a family. In the following chapters, you will hear from trusted authors that represent the voices of those in the church who desire to belong, who value family ministry, yet who often feel displaced in our current church landscape. In this chapter, I will set up the invitation to consider a better way forward and how to get there. But before I do, we must remember where we have been and know where we currently are in this short history of family ministry.

## Where We've Been—Church and Family

While youth ministry has been commonplace in the local church for over fifty years, it has only been within recent decades that family ministry began to be regarded as a legitimate entity. However, when it came to an exact definition of family ministry, one would have been hard-pressed to find a narrow and commonly accepted definition. Definitions may depend on denomination, style, preferences, and theological bent. Despite the recent decade's growth in family ministry organization and models, there is no clear consensus and collaboration on exactly what it is. It has been somewhat of a vacuum for practitioners and organizations to decide as they were led.

Yet, over the last twenty years or so, there have been a couple of clear models that have gained support and traction. The first is the Family-Based model, which represents this idea of "church and family." In family-based churches, the youth, children's, men's, women's, and all ministries continued to be maintained, while organizing periodic opportunities for the generations to get together. Priority is put on training parents through various opportunities, and ministries are responsible for planning and pursuing intentional learning experiences that are designed to draw the generations together.[2] However, much of this is planned individually without collaboration of the entire staff. And for many, the only generational influence encouraged is parent to child. While this model has many strengths, some proponents readily admit this is more a particular ministry philosophy than a model and does not go far enough in addressing the disconnect between the church and the family.[3] It is exceptional at continuing age-segregated programming while somewhat including parental involvement. However, there is a danger of adding more to the already busy schedule of kids and parents' lives, at the risk of losing intentionality. Yet, it was an outstanding start in the movement toward family ministry.

---

[2] Timothy Paul Jones and Randy Stinson, "Family Ministry Models," in Michael and Michelle Anthony (Eds.), *A Theology for Family Ministries* (B&H Publishing Group, 2011), 174.

[3] Paul Renfro, Brandon Shields, and Jay Strother, in T.P. Jones (Ed.), *Perspectives on Family Ministry: Three Views* (B&H Publishing Group, 2009), 98, 129.

## Where We Are—Church With Family

The second model of family ministry has gained popularity over the past several years, and is most likely the most common, practical model to date. This is the Family-Equipping model, which represents the idea of "church with family." Family-equipping practitioners would argue this model moves the needle further than the Family-Based model by equipping parents to be the primary voices in family discipleship. In this model, the partnership between church and home is seen as an interdependent partnership with mutual benefit since neither is fully able to fulfill the job of spiritually forming the next generations alone. Churches who embrace this model often develop benchmarks such as family milestone markers, rites of passage, or church-wide events and recognitions to bring the generations together to encourage parents and model faith formation to the next generations. Many times, these markers and events are preceded by a parenting class that equips them to practice this particular discipline in the home as well as corporately with their local church family.

Strengths of the Family-Equipping model are plentiful, and it is a model that has served the church well in recent years. This model presupposes a unified vision and structure to accomplish its goal. Family-equipping churches enthusiastically co-champion the faith community in partnership with the family, even to a greater degree than family-based churches. If ministries in the local church can align, collaborate with each other, and guard against silos, a church could live effectively in this model. But this is a difficult task in this model. The primacy of traditional, nuclear families can also be elevated with a temptation to become almost idolatrous and thus alienate congregants who do not fit the standard or meet a certain ideal.

## Where We Must Go—Church as Family

While there are clear strengths in each model and movement above, there is a tendency for both to fit their emphases and strengths primarily within the stages of life encompassing childhood and adolescence. There is not much mutual, reciprocal impact between all generations. The focus is primarily on parents and children. A more comprehensive strategy and philosophy must be developed and championed. A strategy that emphasizes and encourages continued spiritual formation and intentional intergenerationality in the stages of adulthood in addition to childhood and adolescence. A model that also encourages an interdependence between all ministries of the church, working together to ensure family discipleship is not just practiced in the home, but corporately as the family of God. That every brother and sister in Christ belongs in the family, not just those who fit the definition of a traditional family. Especially those who feel on the outside—unknown and unseen—yet long to call the church home.

The most common metaphor for the church in the New Testament is *family*; outsiders were welcomed into churches as brothers and sisters.[4] Throughout the Gospels and epistles, it is clear the New Testament church was created and designed to function as a different kind family, a surrogate family of sorts. Status was determined by our shared adoption into the family by Christ and His finished work on the cross, not by bond of blood, marriage, or social standing. This was the intention of Jesus when He formed His new family as we see in Mark 3:31–35:

> Then Jesus' mother and brothers arrived. Standing outside, they sent someone in to call him. A crowd was sitting around him, and they told him,

[4] Steve Bezner, *Your Jesus Is Too American: Calling the Church to Reclaim Kingdom Values Over the American Dream* (Brazos Press, 2024), 10.

> "Your mother and brothers are outside looking for you." "Who are my mother and my brothers?" he asked. Then he looked at those seated in a circle around him and said, "Here are my mother and my brothers! Whoever does God's will is my brother and sister and mother" (NIV).

This was also the intention of Paul and other New Testament writers as they communicated to the early church. Paul used sibling language 118 times, father language 40 times, and inheritance terminology 14 times.[5] He clearly adopted Jesus' model for community, indicated by this extensive use of familial language in his letters. We believe the church today can likewise function in this way, healthy and holistically setting a place at the table for everyone to belong and participate. When the local church views itself as a surrogate kinship group of sorts—a family—it becomes a place where children, teens, parents, families of all kinds, and all generations belong to one another, and generational faith is owned by everyone in the family. And if generational faith transmission was important to the New Testament church, as well as to ancient Israel (Deuteronomy 6:4–9; Psalm 78:3–4, 6), it should be even more crucial for faith communities today.

I have come to the conviction that the future of effective family ministry must include not just the traditional family, but every *kind* of family. Also, not only the families of the church, but also the local, holistic body of Christ, in partnerships and in concert together. To that end, I propose a theological and practical way forward that I pray will challenge and encourage us to rethink and reframe how we organize and practice family ministry.

[5] Joseph Hellerman, *The Ancient Church as Family* (Fortress Press, 2001), 92.

## A Way Forward—Three Pictures and Three Shifts

In addition to the metaphor of family, Paul also called the community of faith "God's household," drawing from strong language and pictures for both Greek and Hebrew traditions and ideas. Ray Anderson acknowledges this new understanding of the church constitutes a new context of belonging as members of God's family and provides a certain self-sufficiency and mutual interdependence to all who belong to it.[6] I like this idea of "household." It brings to memory a home full of our family at holidays. It wasn't necessarily nostalgic, warm and fuzzy all the time, it was mostly chaos. A good chaos. My grandmother, the matriarch of the family, would be cooking Thanksgiving dinner. Aunts, uncles, and cousins, dozens of us, would take over my uncle's home. Craziness would ensue as we were bored and waiting until the meal was ready to be shared. My cousins and I fought as much as we laughed and played. Even the most estranged members of the family were present and welcomed on these special days. It wasn't perfect or pretty; but it was mine, and I miss it to this day. This is what I think of when I hear "God's household." The big, crazy, messy, welcoming family of faith.

If the church is indeed a family and we as leaders in the church are the ones tasked to steward and care for this family, then how do we build this household of faith Paul referred to? I believe we begin by painting three pictures that will help us move toward this new way, this ancient way: a theological picture, a relational picture, and a practical picture that introduces a theoretical new model of family ministry.

[6] Ray Anderson, *Something Old, Something New: Marriage and Family in a Postmodern Culture* (Wipf and Stock Publishers, 2007), 185.

## A Theological Picture: Framing a House

I love home improvement shows. I could watch HGTV and the DIY channel all day long. The operative word is *watch*. I don't think it would turn out well if I attempted to do my own *Farmhouse Fixer* or "yard crash" my own yard! What I love about these shows is that within one hour, one can see the hard work behind the build and finally experience the door opening to new, warm spaces ready to be inhabited and enjoyed by its owners. Reality is that it takes much longer than an hour. In fact, it can take up to several months. In the same way, building an inviting household of faith where all belong and are a part of the family doesn't happen overnight. It takes time. And it must begin with a proper theological understanding of what it means to be a household of faith, the family of God.

My wife and I are experiencing the joys and struggles of renovation firsthand as I write this. This year, we purchased a log cabin on six acres outside of Franklin, Tennessee. For over 20 years, we have had a God-sized dream of one day, in retirement, owning a property where we could host individuals and couples in ministry for a week of rest, renewal, and spiritual direction. In God's kindness He brought about the property and orchestrated the details much earlier than we had hoped or imagined. But it needed work. It was older, only had two tiny bedrooms, one tiny bathroom, a small kitchen, and a very dark, cold, unfinished basement. Over the last year we (and when I say we, I mean the contractors we hired) have gutted the entire main floor and changed the layout, designed and installed a new kitchen, added new hardwood flooring, new walls, added two bathrooms, a new laundry area, designed my study, and finished out the basement, which will be the future ministry area. Apart from a murphy bed and new wood stove, we are done. It took almost a year, but it seems like a lifetime of storage, Pods, and downsizing (oh, did I mention that we lost a ton of square footage in the move?).

Another favorite home improvement show of mine is *Good Bones*, a show about a mother and daughter team that finds old houses in historic neighborhoods with mostly good foundations and framework (the bones) and flips them. I honestly believe our cabin could be on that show. Apart from the inside, it was in outstanding shape. You see, the bones were there, we just needed to reframe things to accomplish the vision and purpose we have for the space.

I believe this is a great picture as we think about moving forward in family ministry and this idea of *church as family*. We are reminded how important the structural integrity of anything we build is key to its sustainability; and this is also true of any program, strategy, or system we build in our churches. This is where we must start. Family ministry has come a long way; it has grown and become a respected ministry in the church. Over the past twenty years, we have seen how it has changed and grown. It is here to stay and is vital. Yet, there is much work to do. It has "good bones," we just need to reframe the conversation to fit the vision and purpose I believe we are called to as we move forward. As we build this theological picture of *church as family*, we begin where most builds do, the foundation. We will then move to the frame that holds and shapes the house. Both the foundation and the framing of a house support the stability and sustainability of the home.

We begin with the foundation, which is the new paradigm of *church as family*. What do we exactly mean by *church as family*? I believe there are three ways to think about this, all from three different theological and practical early influencers of family ministry. First, it models the way Jesus thought of and set up the early church to function—as a surrogate family. Joseph Hellerman, professor of New Testament language and Literature at Biola University, helps us understand this from Jesus' and the first century perspective. He states that when the church is indeed a family, the needs and life of the group take precedence over the individual. This is much of the way Mediterranean families operated in New Testament times. In fact, this is the very structure Jesus had in mind when He formed His church and called them into relationship with one another. Hellerman believes that Jesus calls the Body of Christ, even today, into a new kind of entity where brothers and sisters of all ages (and I would add all kinds of families, all social statuses, all individuals) in the Lord are a new *primary* family.[7] This makes sense when we understand that in Jesus' day and even in the Mediterranean world today, sibling relationships are the strongest of all family ties.

Second, it calls every believer, from 7–70, from the youngest to the oldest, to change the expression of "family" from a thing to an action. I love this because it means we need to make *family* a verb. It is not just something we belong to; it is something we do! Over 40 years ago, before there were even professional youth and family ministries, Dennis Guernsey saw the church as a "family of families" in which the whole of the church functions as family units and therefore adopts and includes those with no proper family system, those unable to have a family, those who've never married, those who've lost spouses or children … you get the picture. He proposed that in our adoption in Christ, we are to "family" one another, especially those with no family or support.[8] Again, it is not just something we are, it is something we *do*.

Third, it requires every ministry to be a part of a holistic family ministry. Diana Garland, pioneer and early voice in family ministry conversations, believed that family ministry is holistic in nature as it involves and depends on the whole of the church community to achieve its purpose. Therefore, family ministry is intentional

[7] For a more comprehensive treatment of Hellerman's contributions, see his two seminal works, *The Ancient Church as Family* (Fortress Press, 2001), and *When the Church Was a Family: Recapturing Jesus' Vision for Authentic Christian Community* (B&H Publishing Group, 2009).

[8] Dennis Guernsey, *A New Design for Family Ministry* (David C. Cook, 1982), 100.

and strategic as it purposely partners with the other ministries of the church to help families live on kingdom mission with Christ.[9]

If the foundation of church as family is the *what*, then the frame of this household of faith is formed by the *why* and the *how*. There are two parts that make up the frame: our adoption in Christ (the why), and intergenerational influence (the how). Adoption in Christ is the first side of the frame. When we mention adoption, it does not mean we "adopt" each other, or that adults "adopt" the young or marginalized. Certainly, this is a part of it, but it is much more comprehensive than that. Instead, we recognize that each one of us have been adopted into the body of Christ, the family of God. In Jesus, we are related to each other; we are siblings, Christian kinfolk (John 1:12; Romans 8:15–17). According to Paul, the Holy Spirit moves believers from slaves of sin into freedom as sons of God, with all the rights and privileges that His Son Jesus Christ enjoys. And Paul fully expected his readers in the local churches to live out this metaphor in their day-to-day relationships. What does this look like today? This theological treatment is also called *adoptive theology*, or *adoptive ministry* and was introduced by Chap Clark, a leading voice in theological work; and Rich's and my theological mentor in seminary. Adoptive ministry is an intentional and strategic process for creating an environment where [everyone in the church] can feel valued and included … where we are all intrinsically connected to one another and partner collaboratively without regard to gifts, function, power, status, or age. Everything we think, do, and plan should enhance those familial relationships.[10]

---

[9] Garland's long-time textbook, *Family Ministry: A Comprehensive Guide* 2ed. (IVP Press, 2012), is replete with these themes throughout.

[10] For a thorough treatment on this line of theological thought, and for a glance into this particular content, check out Chap's book, *Adoptive Theology: Creating an Environment Where Emerging Generations Belong* (Baker Academic, 2018).

The other side of the frame is, the *how*, intergenerational influence. Referenced above, two foundational Scriptures inform the frame of intergenerational influence:

> Listen, O Israel! The LORD is our God, the LORD alone. And you must love the LORD your God with all your heart, all your soul, and all your strength. And you must commit yourselves wholeheartedly to these commands that I am giving you today. Repeat them again and again to your children. Talk about them when you are at home and when you are on the road, when you are going to bed and when you are getting up. Tie them to your hands and wear them on your forehead as reminders. Write them on the doorposts of your house and on your gates (Deuteronomy 6:4-9, NLT).

> We're not keeping this to ourselves, we're passing it along to the next generation—GOD's fame and fortune, the marvelous things he has done. He planted a witness in Jacob, set his Word firmly in Israel, Then commanded our parents to teach it to their children So the next generation would know, and all the generations to come—Know the truth and tell the stories so their children can trust in God, Never forget the works of God but keep his commands to the letter (Psalm 78:4-7, MSG).

In Deuteronomy 6:5–9, God charges His people to remember and practice community principles in their lives with Him, their immediate families, and the community at large. He reminds them of the complete oneness of the triune God in perfect unity and community, and that a call into community relationship with God is a call to love Him with the whole being. Further instructions are given to reach and model this covenant community relationship to the children of the community. Indeed, in the ancient world and mind the task of training and teaching the young was not limited in scope to the maternal parents alone. There was no concept of individualism in ancient times, individuals understood themselves to be part of a greater whole, a community. Likewise in Psalm 78 we see the importance of the community's responsibility to come alongside parents in transmission of faith and "the marvelous things he has done" to the next generation. The expectation was that this model of transmission would continue for generations to come. It was the community's role to "know the truth and tell the stories … never forget the works of God." If this is done well, future generations would know and trust God. In both passages, it is implicit that faith transmission and community is not just for children and families, but for the whole of the community, for everyone. Intergenerational faith formation not only strengthens traditional families, but it also strengthens families of every kind and everyone who desires to call the local church their family and home.

**SM:** *One of the greatest obstacles we face in moving toward "family as a verb" is hyper-individualism. Intergenerational relationships are crucial for the church to flourish because that is how God intended for the faith to be transmitted. Our kids need to grow up in churches where they know they are part of something bigger than just their peer group. What kind of an impact would we make if every person in the church had someone behind them they were leading, someone beside them to share their stage of life experiences, and someone ahead of them who would mentor them and inspire them to live faithful lives?*

## A Relational Picture: Alloparenting

*Alloparenting* is when children are often cared for by parents as well as other individuals, known as *alloparents*. Alloparents can include a broad range of individuals, such as grandparents, elder siblings, relatives, and non-kin (such as teachers, coaches, and mentors) who may provide support. This communal way of raising children has been seen more commonly in African and Asian countries and in non-industrialized, small-scale societies. The presence of kin, particularly grandmothers and older siblings, has been associated with greater child quality of life including social development, cognitive and language ability, educational outcomes, emotional stability and social behavior and adjustment. Closely related is the Japanese concept of *amae*. *Amae* describes not only parent-child relationships but also relationships with spouses, teachers, and other caring people.[11] I believe there is something there ... it does indeed take a community! Not just to raise a child, but to develop a secure base for everyone in the community to belong and participate.

## A Practical Picture: A New Model—Interdependent Family Ministry

What if fostering a sense of community where the church functions as a cohesive family unit wasn't just the job of your family ministry department? What if *every* ministry within the local church took ownership of nurturing the growth and discipleship of the faith family? What if this new paradigm, this new way of thinking about family ministry, changed what it meant to belong to the local church? What if it healed the trauma and hurt that comes with the term "family" for many who are marginalized and not a part of a traditional

[11] Heidi Keller, "Attachment and Culture," *Journal of Cross-Cultural Psychology, 44*(2), (2012), 187.

family, and brought them into a new, healthy understanding of what it means to belong to a community that is greater than themselves? If we follow Jesus, we are members of God's family and must act that way toward one another. I suggest that this new model, this new way of moving forward, can build a deep mutual interdependence among everyone who belongs to the local church!

When we take a more intricate look at what it means to model *interdependent family ministry*, we learn that it doesn't mean we do away with existing environments for kids, students, and even adults. No, it means that we *intentionally work together as ministries in the local church*, across the table from one another, to live into Jesus' call to operate as a family of faith. This forever, eternal family takes precedence over all others, including bloodline. For Jesus, becoming a part of God's church and kingdom meant aligning family allegiances with the Christian's new family. Thus, no matter what type of earthly family one belongs to, or doesn't, they have a safe, secure place where they will always belong and to which they may always come back. This is the central principle of this new way forward I am proposing with interdependent family ministry. It compels every ministry in the local church to be a part of a holistic way of doing family ministry; not just for families as we understand them, but family ministry for everyone in the church, as the collective family of God. In other words, *church as family* means the collective whole, not just a part of the whole. This is what I mean by moving from the way we have always and are currently practicing toward a new way forward. The graphic below might help with a visual of what this could look like. In the diagram, interdependent family ministry happens where each ministry intersects in concert with each other:

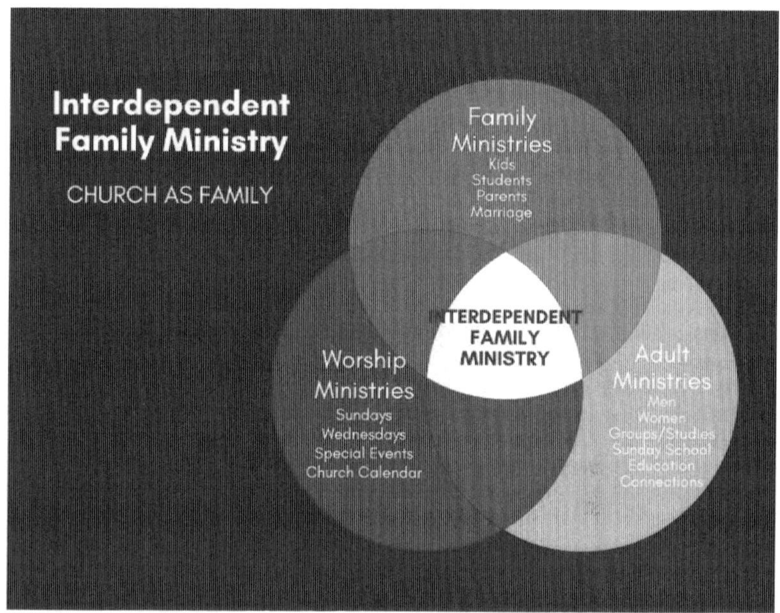


We have already seen Jesus' words in Mark 3 as He began to form this new family of faith. We see another example of this in John 19:25–27, in Jesus' words on the cross just before He died, "Standing near the cross were Jesus' mother, and his mother's sister, Mary (the wife of Clopas), and Mary Magdalene. When Jesus saw his mother standing there beside the disciple He loved, he said to her, 'Dear woman, here is your son.' And he said to the disciple, 'Here is your mother.' And from then on the disciple took her into his home" (NLT). In biblical times with the death of a father or the oldest son, the next oldest brother took care of the widowed mom. Jesus had siblings, but we cannot fully know if they were followers … yet. Why did Jesus not look at James and say this? Was James even there? You see, what Jesus is doing is changing the narrative for His followers from that of their family of blood to a family of faith.

**RG:** *I love the concept of interdependent family ministry! All of the contributing authors acknowledge the continuance and need for affinity-based discipleship opportunities. A sixth-grade-boys group does not need to be engaged in the discussions of a young married small group. This being said, we are not advocating for an entire pendulum swing, rather we are saying some approaches can be seasonal where church as family comes together occasionally for mutual benefit and growth! Intentional intergenerational ministry opportunities certainly reflect "church as family!"*

I like how Ron Hunter, executive director and CEO of D6 Family Ministry puts it. He proposes a change in the definition of family to "people who share a common bond or experience through biological, theological, or relational means." Does this not paint a perfect picture of what it means for the church, in Christ, to be a family and to "family" one another regardless of what constitutes those relationships? He goes on to say that "Family ministry is spiritual ancestry; not stopping at biology but expanding to theology."[12] The common bond we all have as siblings in Christ is and should be what drives how we minister to families and to each other as family. Interdependent family ministry must promote interconnectedness across all church ministries to accomplish this new way of thinking and operating. In this, we nurture mutual relationships with people of all ages. Through this, it cultivates a legacy of faith formation that spans all generations.

But how do we do this, how do we get there? I'll be honest; I do not know of many, if any, churches that are this intentionally collaborative. I do believe this idea is so new it will require a reframing of

[12] Ron Hunter articulated these thoughts during his keynote session at the D6 Conference in Orlando, April 2024.

how we do ministry in the local church. To get to this point, we must address three important shifts in thinking that we must engage.

## Three Shifts in Thinking

One of the biggest challenges you will face will be to reframe the church's role from programs to intentional partnerships and intergenerational relationships within each ministry's sphere of influence as we strive to minister together as staff teams in the local church to develop an environment where everyone belongs, regardless of status. This is that interdependent model we saw earlier. It will look different for each church based on their culture and context. However, to effectively move forward in this new way, it will require three fundamental shifts in our thinking.

First, we must shift from thinking *maternally and paternally* to thinking *eternally.* Most of our family ministry programs and emphases naturally gravitate toward a nuclear, traditional family model. But the early church operated as a family system where Christ and the family of faith took precedence over blood relationships. Instead of planning ministry ***only*** around parents and families, we must begin to plan according to our shared adoption as brothers and sisters in Christ. Now, I am certainly not advocating for doing away with family ministry, kids, and student ministry, nor am I stating a need to abdicate equipping strong, biblical, and traditional families. I am simply advocating for a more holistic ministry that includes, encourages, and equips all members of the local church family. Singles, empty nesters, grandparents, senior adults, college students, co-parenting families, blended families, and divorced singles are all communities that risk feeling marginalized or forgotten when we fail to think in terms of our eternal relationships in addition to our domestic ones. As you begin to engage the rest of this book, you will hear voices from many of these populations, including the traditional nuclear family. We all must work together and be singularly focused this way.

Second, we must shift our thinking from *partnerships* to *partnerships AND relationships.* Over the last several years in family ministry, we have excelled at emphasizing a "partnership" with parents, and indeed this is crucial. Yet, we can still leave the onus of faith formation to them alone, leaving most to feel ill-equipped and all alone in this endeavor. We must make relationships more accessible with those who have traveled this road of faith before us. In our church, we are hearing more and more from young parents who desire to have older parents who are a few steps ahead on the faith trail to speak into their lives. Can you imagine intentional relationships through adult small groups of empty nesters and senior adults with student small groups as they each learn from one another in their own faith journeys?

As churches, we may do well at feeding information, knowledge, and programming to kids, students, and parents; I believe we have fallen short of providing a context of community in which growth, healthy spiritual development, and faith formation can take place with multiple generations learning from one another. Our smaller group environments made up of a multiplicity of folks doing life together as well as generational opportunities are the best, most conducive climates for this to happen together in community.

Which brings us to the third shift in thinking: we must shift from *generational* discipleship alone to also include *intergenerational* discipleship. The term *generational* runs the risk of carrying the notion that all faith formation happens in just the home or through immediate or extended family. It can be a bit exclusive. *Intergenerational* carries an invitation to those outside the immediate family to be an extended faith family for all who call the local church home. It is communal. Intergenerational discipleship can *strengthen* generational discipleship. As parents of all ages and kinds pass and model their own faith journey to the young, they are not alone.

As a church, family is not just something we are, it is something we *do*. Church as family is not only calling dad, mom, and other family members to pass down faith to the next generations but also calls others in the family of faith to share in this important task. In this way, we all own family ministry, not just church staff and parents. All ministries of the local church can work together to ensure faith formation of all generations—not just the next—belongs to every one of us. We must bring the generations together to learn from one another; we are all formed in Christ best in community.

In as much as there is a need to champion this model, there are also threats that could impede or completely shut down an interdependent move to ministry. First, the size of the local church could be a possible threat. Operating as a family in the local church is much easier in smaller congregations, lending itself to organic interdependent ministry. In fact, it is almost a necessity due to staffing and budget limitations. Smaller churches tend to naturally practice intergenerational ministry beyond the worship service, influencing Sunday Schools, small groups, and other specific church programs. In larger and multi-site churches, ministry silos can be a threat. We all have our area we want to protect, and to practice interdependent family ministry most likely will mean giving up something from every ministry department for the sake of our families and our church family. If we are to truly live into this paradigm shift of church as family, we may have to give up some control, leadership, and preference that comes from owning ministry as a staff.

**LF:** *A practical impediment in many churches (especially newer ones) is the layout of facilities. The children's entrance (and hence young families) is on one side of the church; the older adult wing is on the other side. They simply never intermingle unless there* *is a concerted effort to make it happen. In a church I attended recently, some older adults admitted that they did not know a single young person in the church—and the facility design was partly the culprit.*

Another threat to interdependence within the body and church ministries is family trauma. For those who have trauma from their family of origin, using familial language to cast a picture of how we operate as the church can dredge up issues of hurt, trust, pain, and even abuse. How can we care for those in our church family who struggle to think favorably in this way? How can we reframe the narrative around our *Abba* Father and our adoption in Christ and His care for them. We must lead our local churches to be a safe, secure base for them. For many of us, we transfer our view of God from the view of our earthly father. Therefore, for many, family might be a big mess they desire to get away from. However, our adoption in Christ as God's children and our safety in Him redeems the term family for us all!

**RG:** *I am so glad JJ is thinking about the theological implications of adoption. As I write about foster and adoptive families, I was clueless about the effects of trauma on family dynamics and how ill-equipped we often are as churches to address this trauma. As a foster and adoptive parent, I don't expect the church to know how to heal trauma, but I want the church to be a little more understanding of what trauma does to kids. Many of these kids aren't "bad kids," rather they are kids who do not know how to be "the best behaved" because of trauma. I want to remind our readers that the people who are the most difficult to love are the ones who need it the most!*

But where do we start? I suggest you look for your "person of peace." We draw this idea from Jesus' words in Matthew 10:11–14,

> Whatever town or village you enter, search there for some worthy person and stay at their house until you leave. As you enter the home, give it your greeting. If the home is deserving, let your peace rest on it; if it is not, let your peace return to you. If anyone will not welcome you or listen to your words, leave that home or town and shake the dust off your feet (NIV).

Let's be honest: unless we are a senior pastor (and we do hope many of you reading this book are!) we are all leading from the middle and leading when we are not necessarily in charge. How do we reframe the story, the narrative, around what it means to live out church as family? We find that person of peace! That other ministry leader who is like minded or open to thinking strategically and who will welcome us as peacemakers and co-laborers. We find that intersection of our ministry with other ministries and become a bridge. We reach across the table and lead in our ministry areas together in concert with each other.

If you are part of a family ministry staff, children's, or youth staff, what other ministries outside of your area do you have a great relationship with? Who is that ally as you begin to reframe the narrative? Is it your small groups or Sunday School? Maybe empty nesters or boomers? In our church, we are beginning to work toward this. Our boomer's ministry is partnering with our young adult ministry to host and provide seasonal dinners in which each generation invests in the other as they journey in their faith. This includes both singles and married couples from both populations, so that everyone has a voice and is included. Our groups ministry is beginning to talk with our family ministry and dream about what it could look like to partner together and provide group leaders and curriculum for small groups, classes, and studies by developing an age- and life-stage appropriate scope and sequence. Why would we not? The parents we are ministering to make up both of our ministries, it is a shared responsibility. This also ensures we are hearing from *all* parents and their needs, not just from our traditional families.

It will look different in your context than it does in mine. The practical application of church as family is as unique and nuanced as each local church. The key is to start somewhere! Start to make a difference where you can. Take *a* step ... you don't have to take ten steps. Start slowly, pray, have conversations, and reframe the story, and find that one person of peace you can take a small step with. Change the culture of the people in your care, then it will spread.[13]

As the pages of this book continue to unfold, we hope the voices within inspire and challenge readers to think differently, yet more completely about family ministry and what constitutes a "family." We've come a long way in a few short years, and we have great ministries and programs. Yet, how do we call and include everyone in our local churches to embrace and belong to this eternal household of faith? We can and we must! It will take prayer, Spirit dependence, lots of conversations and collaboration, and especially humility.

I am excited and hopeful for the future church, for our leaders that are brave enough to have these important conversations in this book, and for the opportunity before us to finally live into the explicit relationship Jesus has designed for His followers. May we be faithful to this end.

[13] Scott Cormode, YF730, "Leading Change," lecture at Fuller Theological Seminary, Pasadena, CA in 2013.

## Practical Considerations

1. I mention a new way forward for family ministry called "church as family." What excites or intrigues you about this theological shift? What might cause you caution or concern? Of the three shifts mentioned in the chapter, which do you most resonate with? Which might be the most difficult for you or your church?
2. I suggest a new model of family ministry: interdependent family ministry, in which *every* ministry in the church (not just family ministry) owns the discipleship of the family of faith. This includes the church holistically as well as all families in the church. If you were designing a new way forward in your church using this model, how would you design it? What might you do the same and differently? In your ministry context, what are some challenges you might face and what might work?
3. Unless you are a lead pastor, most of us are middle management as ministry leaders. This does not mean we can't begin to make some of these shifts within our sphere of influence. Think about your staff team, who could be that "person of peace" that is like minded and open to this new paradigm? What ministry and leader would be willing to think strategically and collaborate with you?
4. What is one thing that resonated with you in this chapter? What is one, just one, action step you can take to move toward "church as family," even if it is only in your area of ministry?

### References

Anderson, R. *Something Old, Something New: Marriage and Family in a Postmodern Culture.* Wipf and Stock Publishers, 2007.

Clark, C. *Adoptive Theology: Creating an Environment Where Emerging Generations Belong*. Baker Academic, 2018.

Bezner, S. *Your Jesus Is Too American: Calling the Church to Reclaim Kingdom Values Over the American Dream*. Brazos Press, 2024.

Cormode, S. YF730, Leading Change. *Lecture, Fuller Theological Seminary*. Pasadena, CA, 2013.

Demirovic, A. The changing face of American families: A 21st century perspective. *Religions*, 18, (April 2024): 18–31. Retrieved from https://www.proquest.com/scholarly-journals/changing-face-american-families-21st-century/docview/3064706969/se-2.

Garland, D. *Family Ministry: A Comprehensive Guide* (2ed). IVP Press, 2012.

Guernsey, D. *A New Design for Family Ministry*. David C. Cook, 1982.

Hellerman, J. *The Ancient Church as Family*. Fortress Press, 2001.

Hunter, R. keynote presentation D6 Conference, Orlando, FL, 2024.

———. *When the Church Was a Family: Recapturing Jesus' Vision for Authentic Christian Community*. B&H Publishing Group, 2009.

Keller, H. Attachment and Culture. *Journal of Cross-Cultural Psychology, 44*(2), (2012): 187.

Jones, T.P. and R. Stinson. Family Ministry Models. In M. & Mc. Anthony (Eds.), *A Theology for Family Ministries*. B&H Publishing Group, 2011.

*Parenthood*. "Because You're My Sister," Season 4, episode 15. Originally aired January 22, 2013.

Renfro, P., B. Shields, and J. Strother. In T.P. Jones (Ed.), *Perspectives on Family Ministry: Three Views*. B&H Publishing Group, 2009.

## Chapter 2

# Engaging and Equipping Single Parent Families

Shelly Melia, Ph.D.

I am a planner. I get as much joy from planning vacations as I do from taking them. And it's not just vacations; I love planning my life. For the first 35 years of my life, I felt blessed to see most of those plans and dreams come true. After college, I married my husband, and five years later, we started our family, eventually welcoming three beautiful children. I loved watching my husband in his role as a dad. He was "all in" when it came to parenting our children. Everything was falling into place for our little family of five until June 16, 2005.

I was the children's minister at our church, and we were in the middle of Vacation Bible School. I left the house early that morning as a wife, mom, and children's minister, ready for a full day of VBS. Later that afternoon, I returned to my home with a new identity. I was now a widowed, single parent. I was 35 years old, and our children were just six, four, and two years old when my husband was killed in a car accident. Being a single parent was not something I ever imagined for myself. It was not part of my plan, and I struggled to understand how it could be a part of God's good plan for my life.

**LF:** *Shelly, your personal journey adds so much credibility to this chapter!*

Every single parent's story is unique. But there are at least two things most single parents have in common: they did not plan to be single parents, and their journey almost always includes pain or trauma. One single mom said, "Nobody becomes a single parent because that is a burning desire deep in their soul." While single parents may not have planned to be single parents, the church must develop plans to better minister to single parents and their children.

In full transparency, before June 2005, I was focused on my family, surrounded by two-parent families, and had no concept of what it meant to experience life as a single parent. Regrettably, as the children's minister at our church, I had a voice at staff meetings, but single parents were not on my radar. I certainly had compassion, but my effectiveness in advocating for and ministering to them was lacking. Now, after almost twenty years of being one myself, perhaps the most gracious way to state where I was and where I have observed most churches missing the mark in ministering to single parents is to acknowledge "we don't know what we don't know."

**RG:** *Shelly makes a great point here worth reiterating: We cannot have true empathy with any individual or group until we have experienced what they have experienced. I thought I was a great youth pastor… until I became a parent! In the past I have stated—especially regarding being a single and adoptive parent—"If a person can't have empathy, I would settle for sympathy because that sure beats apathy!" If we haven't experienced life from the perspective of a "fifth wheel family," we should at least engage in conversations that get to know them and their perspective.*

This chapter aims to help pastors and ministry leaders "know what they need to know" to minister more intentionally to single parents. The assumption is there is a desire to reach and disciple this growing population (Matthew 28:19–20) and a willingness to consider a perspective unfamiliar to most pastors and ministry leaders. We will unpack these three questions as we consider the needs of single-parent families in our churches and communities:

1. Do you see me?
2. Do I belong here?
3. Do you need me?

Testimonials are included within each section to bring content to life and provide insight and understanding into what single parents experience in their local churches. (Side note: The testimonies in this chapter come from single parents who actively serve, give, and attend faithfully in their local church).

## Statistics

Statistics on single parents are ubiquitous, and this chapter will not attempt to address current data fully. Pew Research (2019) and the Census Bureau (2022) provide data pertinent to the faith community as we consider the prevalence of single parents in our churches and communities:

- Almost 1 in 4 children live in a single-parent home in the United States (Pew, 2019)
- Only 7% of the world's children live in single-parent homes. This means children in the United States are three times more likely to live in a single-parent home than anywhere else in the world (Pew, 2019)
- Single mothers maintain 80% of single-parent families (US Census, 2022)

An emerging trend that will eventually significantly impact communities and churches is the increase in births outside of marriage. According to a report from The Forum on Child and Family Statistics, *America's Children: Key National Indicators of Well-Being*, 40% of all births in 2021 were to unmarried women. The category of 20–24-year-old women came in with the highest rate of births to unmarried women at 68%. Let that sink in for a moment: 68% of babies born to 20–24-year-old mothers in 2021 were *not* born into a traditional family. It is not enough to be pro-birth and support local pregnancy aid centers; we must be prepared to be pro-life for the entire life of the mother and the child. The church has generations of work to keep the long-term commitment required to be fully pro-life.

The potential adverse outcomes for children raised in single-parent households have long been part of the research narrative. These outcomes are typically described in terms of socioeconomic disparity, mental health struggles, academic barriers, attachment and abandonment issues, substance abuse, and even negative health outcomes. The needs of children in single-parent homes cannot be understated. Who better than the church to stand in the gap for children growing up in single-parent homes?

## Stop and Consider

- Which statistics stick out to you as most significant for the church to understand or address?
- What ministries in our local churches could address the potential adverse outcomes the children of single parents experience?
- When mothers choose life, how can the church stand in the gap and minister to both the parent and child for the long haul?

## Do You See Me?

One of the greatest needs of single parents is to be seen. The Old Testament story of Hagar, found in Genesis 16, provides biblical support for the importance and impact of being seen. The story is too complex to unpack here completely, but the message is simple: God saw Hagar's pain. Hagar had little control over her life circumstances. She did not plan to be pregnant by someone who was not her husband, and she was certainly experiencing a lot of shame and pain.

Hagar, an enslaved Egyptian, ran away from the cruelty she experienced at the hands of Sarai. Alone in the desert, the Angel of the Lord came to her and spoke to her. In Genesis 16:13, Hagar did something no other person in the Old Testament did. She gave God the name *El-Roi* or "The God who sees." Hagar goes on to say, "I have now seen the One who sees me" (NIV). Hagar was not invisible to God, and knowing God saw her pain changed her outlook, allowing her to embrace God's purpose for her life, even when it was not what she had planned or deserved.

Do. You. See. Me? Reading the story of Hagar gives more context to why this question is a focus of this chapter. How could we *not* see the increasing numbers of single parents in our churches and communities? If we are paying attention to what is happening in our world, we know the numbers are rising. So why is there even a question about whether we see them? The answer may surprise you: Single parents often carry shame, they may wonder if God sees their pain, and they are not sure the church truly sees them. To see someone as God saw Hagar is to see their pain and choose to focus on the person and their purpose rather than their circumstances, some of which they may have had no control over.

How can the church do a better job of seeing them? Listen to their stories, not to fix them or even to determine who is to blame for their circumstances. Listen to understand their story. Consider the perspective of these single parents as they describe ways in which they have not always felt seen in church settings.

> "Sunday was always the loneliest day of my week. Whether it was my perception or not, I always felt alone and second class at church." (LR)
>
> "In all my years of attending church, I haven't heard a sermon affirming or honoring single parents. By default, I am the spiritual leader in my home, and I could use some encouragement from time to time. I know I cannot provide all the things my children need, but I am doing the best I can. Sometimes, I wish my pastor would speak some life and hope into my life as a single mom." (LM)
>
> "Sadly, people's biases can play a significant role in the assumptions they make about us. We may be seen as reckless instead of responsible, sinful instead of lost and struggling, or that our current circumstances result from our choices rather than the repercussions of someone else's choices." (MH)

Two thought leaders in single-parent ministry, who were also single parents at one time and went on to lead significant single-parent family ministries in their churches and communities, provide valuable insight into understanding the needs of single parents. First, Linda Jacobs, author of *The Single-Parent Confident and Successful* and creator of Divorce Care for Kids (DC4K.org):

> Single parents need extra reassurance that they are valued by God and the church. The feelings of rejection and abandonment from a former spouse or parent of their child can be raw and overwhelming, and they can be extra sensitive to anything that feels like rejection or abandonment by the church as well.

Next, Dawn VanderWerf, co-author of *The Daddy Gap,* offers practical and specific suggestions for pastors and ministry leaders:

> Speak to them directly in Sunday services. Acknowledge their suffering, their financial struggles, and their unique and difficult calling, and affirm them for their courage in parenting and spiritually leading their family alone. Receiving public acknowledgment and encouragement from male church leaders is incredibly powerful and costs nothing!

If you are still with me, you may be feeling conflicted about these testimonies and suggestions. For some, elevating the needs of single parents could signal a retreat from fidelity to the biblical ideal: a two-parent family. Before becoming a single parent, I might have even interpreted the testimonies as "negative" or "needy." I had good intentions, but there were significant gaps in my understanding of what it meant to be a single parent. Without meaning to, I prioritized the needs of two-parent families while overlooking and sometimes misunderstanding the needs of my brothers and sisters in Christ who were experiencing life as a single parent. I did not truly see their struggles and discouragement, even while at church.

Striking a balance between upholding the biblical ideal of a two-parent family while also seeking to help non-single pastors, ministry leaders, and parents consider what they might not know about the perspective and needs of single parents is a tightrope to walk carefully. This chapter is not about devaluing the traditional, two-parent family as the desired norm for families in our churches. Dr. Kevin Jones' chapter on the traditional family does a beautiful job of emphasizing the importance of this biblical ideal. Instead, this chapter aims to shine the light on our blind spots so we "know what we need to know" and so we can make plans to "do what needs to be done" to reach single-parent families.

### Stop and Consider

- What blind spots did this chapter reveal as you considered the need for single parents to be seen?
- Does your church speak directly to single parents from the pulpit? What small step could you take in speaking hope and life into single parents?
- Which of the testimonies spoke to you? What assumptions do you often make about single parents?

## Do I Belong?

Belonging is a primary pain point for all of us, but especially for single parents. Lack of belonging manifests itself in loneliness and isolation. The U.S. Surgeon General's recent report on the mental health and well-being of parents found that 77% of single parents experience loneliness (Surgeon General report, 2023). Even though technology and social media provide ample avenues for connection, "single parents often feel isolated or marginalized within their communities" (Table for One Ministries, 2024).

Belonging is the gateway for single parents to experience genuine biblical community with fellow believers. Throughout Scripture, the importance of relationships and biblical community is emphasized. In the creation story, God declared it was not good for man to be alone (Genesis 2:18), underscoring the need for connection. In Deuteronomy 6:5–7, in addition to the instructions given to parents, the entire community of faith was expected to reach and teach children collectively (Hunter, 2025). Moving to the New Testament, Acts 2:42–47 describes the early church not as consumer-driven but as a collective community of faith: "They devoted themselves to the apostles' teaching and to fellowship, to the breaking of bread and to prayer" (Acts 2:42, NIV).

**JJ:** *Shelly brings up an excellent point. Simply because adults have experienced individuation does not mean we do not struggle with belonging. There is a growing body of evidence that suggests attachment continues on into adulthood and "secure bases" of relationships are just as important during adulthood as they are during childhood and adolescence. We ALL desire to have a secure base we can belong to in safety. It stands to reason that for all believers the church, the family of God, should and could provide the best space for belonging. As a current groups pastor, I have seen firsthand how small groups can provide a place for single parents to belong and contribute to the church without judgment or embarrassment. I have seen intergenerational groups that include and welcome families and parents of all circumstances. Groups are a simple, easy onramp for* ***everyone*** *to belong.*

The importance of belonging for single parents cannot be overstated. Without belonging, single parents are unable to experience biblical community. To bring the concept of belonging to life, consider two seemingly unrelated images: elephants and bridges. Picture a group of mama elephants moving together in the wild. Next, envision a massive bridge that provides connection and access where none existed before.

## Mama Elephants

First, the mama elephants. If you were in the wild observing mama elephants, you might notice some interesting behaviors. For example, when a mama elephant is about to give birth to a baby elephant, there are certain things other mama elephants in the herd do. Mama elephants circle around the vulnerable elephant and close ranks as she prepares to give birth. They kick up dust to throw off predators and stand together in solidarity to protect the mama elephant while she does the life-giving work of birthing her baby. Once the baby is born, the mama elephants trumpet loudly to celebrate the new life.

I host a women's Bible study group in my home, and we affectionately call our group "the elephants." When I need support, my elephants are there for me. They pray for me, kick up dirt to protect me when I am vulnerable, and maybe, most importantly, celebrate with me when good things happen. I cannot imagine my life as a single parent without the support and love of my elephants. They have stood beside me in times of great sorrow and struggle, prayed me through worries and fears, and are the first to throw a party when there is a reason to celebrate.

My experience as a single parent finding my "herd" is likely more the exception than the rule. I had the benefit of being on staff at our church, and finding belonging was not as challenging as it is for people who come into a community of faith without anyone knowing them or their stories. After a divorce, single parents often lose their sense of belonging due to no longer fitting into the married groups they once enjoyed. A quick look at almost any church website that lists Bible study groups will reveal that the choices for single parents are limited to non-existent, while the lists for married adult groups are extensive.

What is the proverbial elephant in the room? Very few churches make single-parent ministry a mission-critical ministry of the church. There are likely many reasons for this, but here are a few possibilities: Some churches do not identify single-parent families as their target audience, others may not believe single-parents will be a good return on their investment, or perhaps there are even churches who have unintentionally made marital status a barrier for belonging. Acknowledging the diversity in family structures is essential for creating a church environment where belonging can open the door for biblical community to flourish.

## Bridges

Now, turn your attention to the massive bridge in your mind. Bridges allow people to get somewhere they could not go without the bridge. Bridges are necessary to move people across large bodies of water, through massive canyons, or just from one side of a busy highway to another. What would happen if there were suddenly no bridges? In many places, the lack of bridges would create isolation, and natural barriers would cut off people from essential resources.

What do bridges have to do with belonging for single parents? Think about your church. Are there bridges single parents can easily cross to find their "herd" and experience belonging that leads to biblical community? Or do single parents in your church run into more barriers than bridges, resulting in isolation and loneliness? Are there clearly marked paths to finding biblical community, regardless of their marital status? Is the language used from the pulpit and in publications inclusive of more than just the two-parent family? When ministry events happen at the church, is childcare provided for parents who do not have another dependable adult in the house? For single parents, childcare is often a critical bridge that must be in place for them to participate in the programs and ministries of the church. Below is a compilation of experiences of single parents who either found it challenging to access bridges to belonging and biblical community in their church or experienced hurt when people in the church missed opportunities to step into their child's pain and maintain strong bridges for belonging:

> "When I was a single mom, my church offered a parenting class, and when I went online to register, the system would not let me proceed with the next registration step without listing my spouse's name. Fortunately, I was cre-

ative and listed Jesus as my spouse, so when I showed up to the class there was a nametag for me and Jesus! While I don't believe the leaders had any intention of excluding me or any other single parents from participating, there are still systems like this in place in many churches that unknowingly exclude single parents from being included in many activities." (DV)

"I wish churches would take steps to ensure single parents feel genuinely welcomed and valued. Many single parents avoid church out of fear of judgment or a sense of not belonging. Most programs are tailored to traditional family structures, leaving those who have a family that looks different from that feeling excluded. By recognizing this, churches can create an environment where every family feels they truly belong." (MK)

"Language is critical. For example, using the term "broken home" to describe single parent families does not communicate hope or belonging. Remember, all people are broken, not just single parents." (SM)

"It is hard for a single parent to feel included. I hate going anywhere and sitting or eating by myself. Some weekends, you might have your child(ren), and the next week, they might be with their ex-spouse. It is hard to attend church when single and without someone else accompanying you. It is also hard on the child(ren) to attend one week and miss the other." (MM)

"When I was a single mom at a small church, nobody did anything. We missed a few weeks in a row, and no one called. My daughters were in the youth group; they shared with the leaders what was happening at home, but no one showed up for them, not one person." (DC)

> "My child's father was a deacon, sang on the praise team, and taught Sunday School. He left us because of an affair. The youth pastor prayed with my daughter one time at a disciple now event three months after he left and that was all the care she ever received from the church. The youth pastor knew the whole story because her dad was one of the teachers." (RL)

What about when churches get it right? Here are some stories from single parents who found belonging and a biblical community in their churches. What is the common denominator? There were bridges already in place for them. Do you know what else is impressive about their stories? Each one of the single parents below has gone on to become a bridge-building specialist, doing even more for other single parents than what was done for them. In each case below, the person has spent over twenty years dedicating their time and resources to lead and equip single-parent ministries nationwide. You never know who may cross the bridge you build or how God will use their pain for His glory.

> "When I was a single mother, I found a church that hosted a single-parent support group once a week. They welcomed me and my children, providing meals and childcare while I attended Bible study. They also adopted our family for Christmas, gifting us with a brand-new winter coat. I felt loved." (MK)
>
> "I am thankful that the church the Lord led me to knew what to do with me. They were ready (30 years ago). They placed me in a biblical community that surrounded me with friendship, fellowship, and prayer. They helped guide me and welcomed me in with open arms." (HC)
>
> "I had no funds for presents that first year I was raising my kids on my own. Someone in our church found out, and on Christmas Eve, they came over after the kids were in bed,

> and they brought in presents for each of us. The presents were all wrapped and with each person's name on a card. That wonderful family of God continued walking along beside us. The men invited my young son on a fishing trip. One lady brought us a meal on Friday evening. It was just mac and cheese, Jello, and green beans, but it spoke volumes to my children that God's people loved us." (LJ)
>
> "As we were developing the ministry, there was a very significant thing that happened that seemed insignificant but was really very large and could be the crux of the matter … it was calling them family. If you ask anyone in a single-parent family if they feel like a family, they resoundingly say 'YES.' However, the American church does not always view them as a family. So, instead of a single-parent ministry, we always say it's a 'Single-parent FAMILY Ministry.' This seems insignificant, but in reality, they want to know they are legitimately a part of a family, a church family, and truly belong." (HC)

One final word about bridges: bridges are built over time. Sometimes, they take years to build, but the benefits are multi-generational. When we communicate through both word and deed that we truly see single parents and take the time to intentionally and sacrificially build bridges for them to experience belonging and biblical community, then we will begin to see the transformation and healing God offers through the experience of knowing Him and being loved and cared for by His people.

> "With God and a healthy biblical community, healing begins and almost always is not a long road … but one that He will set out for each family to bring true restoration." (leader of a single-parent ministry for 16 years)

### Stop and Consider

- How has your perspective of single parents been enlarged by reading the testimonies of single parents? Which story resonated with you the most?
- What comes to mind that you might be able to do to ensure that single parents have access to bridges to belonging in your church?

## Do You Need Me?

Being "needed" is a biblical concept, and single parents have an important role to play in the body of Christ. God designed the Church to function as a body, with each part of the body fulfilling an important role. In 1 Corinthians 12:18–26 Paul taught us about the importance of interdependence:

> But in fact God has placed the parts in the body, every one of them, just as he wanted them to be. If they were all one part, where would the body be? As it is, there are many parts, but one body.
>
> The eye cannot say to the hand, "I don't need you!" And the head cannot say to the feet, "I don't need you!" **On the contrary, those parts of the body that seem to be weaker are indispensable,** and the parts that we think are less honorable we treat with special honor. And the parts that are unpresentable are treated with special modesty, while our presentable parts need no special treatment. But God has put the body together, giving greater honor to the parts that lacked it, so that there should be no division in the body, but that its parts should have equal concern for each other. If

> one part suffers, every part suffers with it; if one part is honored, every part rejoices with it" (NIV, emphasis added).

Did you catch verse 22 (emphasized above)? Go back and reread it. What does it say about the "weaker parts" of the body? They are *indispensable*! Joni Eareckson Tada, the founder of Joni and Friends ministry, often describes effective disability ministry in this way: "It is not a disability ministry until the disabled are ministering." According to Tada, not only should churches be prepared to minister to those who are disabled, but churches should also encourage and empower those who are disabled to live out God's purpose for their lives by serving and ministering to others. What if we applied that same principle when we measured the effectiveness of ministry to single parents?

*It is not a single-parent ministry until the single parents are ministering.*

Indeed, single-parent families often have significant needs. Some need financial assistance, while others struggle emotionally or spiritually. Recovery from trauma, abuse, abandonment, or addiction may also be a part of their journey and take time to navigate fully. However, a significant aspect of healing for the single parent is to find their purpose (to be needed) and make meaning from their pain. Churches often underestimate the contribution single parents can make:

> "The biggest myth is that single-parent families will consume and drain the resources of the church, primarily the staff's time and the church's finances. Yet, with God, the single-parent family will not only heal with a healthy biblical community but will grow and mature spiritually, eventually leading to contributions back into the church and healthy families." (HC)

> "When I was a single mom, my church did a great job of making sure I knew I wasn't disqualified because I was divorced or less useful to God because I was single. They invited me into serving and leadership opportunities, giving me a sense of purpose and belonging during some of my most difficult seasons." (DV)

This section, which highlights the importance of single parents discovering their purpose and contributing to the local church's mission, will likely resonate deeply with pastors and ministry leaders. A significant challenge many local churches face is moving members—whether single or married—to transition from consumers to active contributors. However, it is crucial to recognize that most single parents will not make this shift unless they feel "seen" and experience a sense of belonging that draws them into biblical community.

### Stop and Consider

- Are the single parents in your church given opportunities and encouraged to use their gifts? Do you invite them to the leadership table to hear their perspective and benefit from their experiences?
- Do you agree with this statement: "It is not a single parent ministry until single parents are ministering? Why or why not?

## Practical Considerations

Now that you "know what you need to know," how do you "do what needs to be done?" Where does a church begin when trying to address the needs of single-parent families? Here are a few general principles:

1. No universal plan or program for ministering to single parents will work in every context. Be Spirit-led rather than pro-

gram-driven. Spend considerable time in prayer, asking God to reveal the work He is calling you to do.

2. Start small and know your primary purpose: reaching single-parent families with the gospel. By starting small, you are more likely to sustain the ministry. Determine in advance to train and replicate leaders before expanding the ministry. Too many single-parent ministries have started with a bang, only to eventually die because they were unsustainable.
3. Include single parents in the conversation about ministry to them. Give them a voice and a seat at the table. Tell them they are needed (and wanted!) and equip and empower them to use their gifts.
4. Ask hard questions and solicit honest feedback about the current state of your church's ministry to single parents. Be willing to listen to the answers of single parents, even when it is hard to hear.
5. Do your homework on potential support group curriculums and programs that may be needed to assist single parents in the healing and recovery process. If your church cannot start a support group, find one nearby and refer single parents from your church.

Special consideration for ministering to the children of single parents:

1. Find ways to be more inclusive of the children in activities that rely on the presence of both parents in the home. For example, if your church has a father-daughter banquet or a mother-son event, ask single parents how you can best include their children. There is not one solution that is right for every family. Some will be happy for another dad to include their daughter in the event. For others, it may not be practical, or the child may feel uncomfortable going with someone they

do not know well. The most important thing is to communicate to the single parent an understanding this event is challenging for their child to participate in (you see them), and you want to be someone who fills in the gap for them (you will help them experience the church "as family"). The worst thing you can do is say nothing or assume the child is oblivious that they are missing out. Children feel left out when they see their friends getting to do things they cannot do. One single parent shared that her daughter did not want to go to church during the weeks leading up to the father-daughter banquet because she saw the posters and announcements for it, which made her sad. She avoided church because of the pain of not having her father there to take her to an important event (prior to the divorce, her dad always took her).

2. Use language in sermons and other contexts that communicate an understanding of the different family contexts parents and children find themselves in. I always notice when a pastor talks about the father being the spiritual leader of the home. I often wonder what goes through the minds of children who hear this but do not have a father to take on this role. I have never heard a pastor explain what a single or widowed mom should do when there is no father in the home to be the spiritual leader. The reality is that all parents should spiritually lead their children because the world is already discipling them away from the things of God.
3. Consistently speak hope into the lives of single parents and their children. There. Is. Hope. Single-parent families are not second-class, and their children are not destined to turn out poorly. Kids from single-parent families can experience the same transformational gospel as kids from two-parent families. God can do amazing work in any family. Need an example? Consider D. L. Moody. His father died when he was only

four years old, and his mother never remarried. Moody went on to become one of the greatest evangelists of all time. Dr. Ben Carson and C. S. Lewis also found themselves as young children in a single-parent home with less-than-ideal circumstances. Never underestimate the plan God has for children of single parents. Be part of their story of hope, salvation, and restoration through the local church.

4. Recognize the need for mentors in the lives of the children of single parents. Some churches may have the resources to develop formal mentoring ministries, but most churches need a simpler and more organic approach. Consider this story from a volunteer in a single mom's ministry:

   "Christ-following men are needed to step in. Example: I had a man who let me know that he was unable to help with our older kids (he had been an incredible volunteer in the past) because his grandson had games on Wednesday nights; I suggested that he take one of the kids who had outgrown our children's ministry with him to watch his grandson's game. He had never thought of that and said, 'Sure! I can do that!' Moms and dads do not have to miss out on their family things; just incorporate another child in! It also gives the mom a break, AND your kids will learn from your Christ-like example! It really is a win-win-win!" (AB)

5. Prioritize safety and ensure policies are in place to conduct background checks on any volunteer with minors. Require volunteers to complete training in sexual abuse awareness and insist volunteers follow ministry guidelines related to best practices in children's and student ministries. An adult should never be alone with a minor for any amount of time.

## Concluding Thoughts

Chapter One introduced a paradigm shift: moving from an over-reliance on the traditional family structure for implementing family ministry to a model rooted in the ancient (and biblical) practices of interdependence and intergenerational discipleship. For single parents, this shift significantly increases the likelihood of experiencing the church as their primary place of belonging.

As the testimonies throughout this chapter revealed, one of the most significant challenges a single parents faces is the struggle to feel a true sense of belonging. This often prevents them from finding their "herd" and fully experiencing the church as a family.

Dr. PJ Dunn, founder of Table for One Ministries, notes it is not enough to be welcoming, churches must fully include single parents:

> Imagine being invited to a feast, only to be escorted to a folding table in the corner with plastic cups and leftover décor. Too often, this is how single adults feel in church spaces—welcomed, but not fully included. They may be offered a ministry "table," but it's often separated, minimized, or temporary.[1]

However, this longing for belonging is not limited to single parents. According to research in *Growing Young* by the Fuller Youth Institute, one of the most common phrases young people used to describe thriving churches was that they felt "like family."

If current statistics are any indication, growing churches must prioritize addressing the needs of single parents—or risk missing the opportunity to reach more than 50% of the families in their communities. By engaging with the three questions outlined in this chapter, churches can shift toward a more comprehensive model of family

[1] PJ Dunn, Table for One Ministries. tfoministries.org. https://tfoministries.org/does-your-church-still-have-a-kids-table-for-singles-its-time-to-rethink-single-adult-ministry.

ministry, where single parents not only experience the church *as family* but also actively contribute to it. When single parents experience the church as their family, it will transform family from something they simply belong to into something they actively do.

**References**

*ChildStats.gov – America's Children: Key National Indicators of Well-Being, 2023 – Births to Unmarried Women.* (n.d.). https://www.childstats.gov/americaschildren/family2.asp.

Dunn, PJ. Table for One Ministries. tfominstries.org. https://tfoministries.org/does-your-church-still-have-a-kids-table-for-singles-its-time-to-rethink-single-adult-ministry.

Hunter, R. Generational Discipleship Among Spiritual Orphans. In K. Kennemur, K. King, S. Melia & D. Peavey (Eds.), *Children and Salvation: Biblical, Spiritual, and Practical Considerations.* B&H Academic, 2025.

Jacobs, Linda Ranson. *The Single Parent: Confident and Successful.* Bethany House, 2019.

Kent, D. (2024, April 14). U.S. has world's highest rate of children living in single-parent households. *Pew Research Center.* https://www.pewresearch.org/short-reads/2019/12/12/u-s-children-more-likely-than-children-in-other-countries-to-live-with-just-one-parent/.

Ministries, T. for O. (2024, October 12). *Why National Single-Parents Day Should Matter to the Church.* Table for One Ministries – Singles Ministry, Conference, Bible Study. https://tfoministries.org/why-national-single-parent-day-should-matter-to-the-church.

U.S. Census Bureau. (2024, April 4). *Census Bureau Releases New Estimates on America's Families and Living Arrangements.* Census.gov. https://www.census.gov/newsroom/press-releases/2022/americas-families-and-living-arrangements.html.

U.S. Surgeon General. (2024). "Parents Under Pressure." hhs.gov. https://www.hhs.gov/sites/default/files/parents-under-pressure.pdf.

Walker, D., & Haviland, M. *The Daddy Gap*. Westbow Press, 2014.

## Chapter 3

# Engaging and Equipping Grandparents

Larry Fowler

He approached me at a break in the Grandparenting Matters seminar that I was teaching. As he walked up to where I was standing, I was impressed with his immaculate head of silvery-white hair (especially because God didn't give me that gene). He was smartly dressed, and I immediately got the impression of a refined, successful gentleman. But as he got closer, I could see that his face was flushed, and his eyes were a little red.

"Let me introduce myself," he began. "I am the chairman of the board of elders at this church. I have served in about every ministry there is here, gone on mission trips, taught many classes." Then emotion entered his voice:

"Why has it never occurred to me to have a ministry with my own grandkids? How could I have missed this?"

That chairman of the board of elders represents the vast majority of church leaders—very few have ever considered the grandparent-grandchild relationship as deserving of attention, time, and resources.

## The State of Grandparenting in the Church

Grandparenting is simply the most overlooked, under-resourced, and misunderstood relationship within the family, yet it has incredible potential for discipling the youngest generations. Please consider each of the following points more fully.

### Most Overlooked

In 2016, when we launched the Legacy Coalition, we were not able to find a single church in America that was attempting to equip grandparents on even a semi-regular basis. That number is much different now, but more on that later. Many pastors have told me, "I'm a grandparent myself, but it's never occurred to me to preach on the topic."

No church worth its salt would ignore parents and their role in discipleship; the importance of encouraging them and equipping them to disciple in the home is universally accepted by church leaders. I believe 99% of pastors would know they need to provide biblical instruction for parents; but I also believe that 99% of churches have done little to equip grandparents.

### Most Under-Resourced

When we started our ministry, we looked for resources created between the year 2000 and 2016: we could only find one book published by a publisher on the role of a Christian grandparent. About a half-dozen more were self-published but had very limited distribution. When it came to printed resources for grandparents, the bookshelf was bare. There was only one video series on the role. The shortfall was simply startling. The Christian community at large—and the church—have had a blind spot in looking at discipleship in the family; and that blind spot is the role of grandparents.

**RG:** *As someone who has spoken at a number of grandparent camps, another way grandparents are under-resourced is that they are often on fixed incomes! This is a challenge for grandparents who are raising grandchildren. With church as family, we might need to consider being more aware of partnering with grandparents to make sure these kids can go to camp, on mission trips or—better yet—save some money by creating "church as family" camps. This is a great way to more intentional intergenerational church!*

## Misunderstood

"Oh, we've already got a senior adult ministry." I can't count the times I've heard that response from church leaders when I asked them about ministering to grandparents. But a grandparent ministry is not synonymous with senior adult ministry:

First, most grandparents are not senior adults. The average age a person becomes a grandparent in the United States is estimated at around 50.[1] Various estimates put the average age of a grandparent from 60 to 65, giving confirmation to the startling reality that more grandparents now are Gen Xers than boomers. Since most senior adult ministries in the church focus on those 70 and older, "grandparents" are simply a different—and much wider—age strata than "senior adults."

Second, younger grandparents especially—but also those in their sixties—don't want to be called "senior adults." Qualifying for Medicare is an uncomfortable insult to many; they revel in their health

[1] "Grandparents Today National Survey," p.3, AARP, https://www.aarp.org/content/dam/aarp/research/surveys_statistics/life-leisure/2019/aarp-grandparenting-study.doi.10.26419-2Fres.00289.001.pdf.

and vitality and have no desire to be part of that older group, which is composed more of great-grandparents than it is of grandparents.

> **JJ:** *Thank you, Larry! As a newer grandparent myself, (my wife and I just welcomed our second grandchild!) I certainly do not want to be equated with the senior adults in our church—we are still in our fifties even though we are grandparents. We are active, mobile, and entering into our most productive years of ministry. In fact, I still feel like a 25-year-old youth pastor in my mind! Though I am a Gen-Xer and not a boomer generationally, I do know even the "boomers" (born 1964 and earlier) do not wish to be lumped in with senior adults. Many of the boomers of our church are high leadership professionals, business owners, and entrepreneurs; all while being grandparents. What a gift for our generations to have even more time and resources to leave a legacy of faith to our kids and grandkids.*

Third, a senior adult ministry is usually about *ministering to* those in the group. That often looks like hymn sings, potlucks, group trips, hospital visits, and too many funerals. But a grandparent ministry is focused on getting grandparents *to minister*, specifically, in their family. It does not have to do with an age stratum in the church (after all, grandparents can be ages 35 to 105), but rather about a family relationship and a family responsibility.

The comment from the board of elders chairman is worth repeating: "How could [we] have missed this?

If your church has missed it, the rest of the chapter is focused on building a philosophical foundation for having a grandparenting component to your church ministry. You will learn four principles that address the "why" of a grandparenting ministry:

1. The Bible mandates the involvement of grandparents in perpetuating faith in families.
2. There is great potential for the discipleship of the youngest generations through the grandparent-grandchild relationship.
3. The dangers of the dominant cultural view of a "good" grandparent hinder the advancement of the kingdom of God.
4. The church's health and mission are benefited by focusing the attention of the older third of their congregation on passing on faith in their families.

## The Biblical Mandate

I didn't know the Bible said anything about the grandparent role. My Bible college and seminary education never mentioned it. I had spent decades in a very Scripture-focused children's ministry (Awana), but I never saw it. When my first grandson was born, I was so excited to welcome him into our family, but I never had a single thought remotely close to "As a grandfather, what does God have for me to do?"

Then, as part of my role as one of the executive leaders of Awana, I was required to study the passages in the Old Testament that spoke of generations. It was part of a curriculum project that never went anywhere, but God used that study to help me begin to see my grandparent role (and Scripture) with new eyes.

### Where Is Grandparenting in the Bible?

I learned that the word "grandparent" doesn't appear in Scripture. Gender-specific words, however, do occur. We know of Timothy's grandmother Lois (2 Timothy 1:5) and her influence on her grandson. The word, "grandfather" appears just a few times in modern translations. And when it does appear it simply is a relationship identifier, as in 2 Samuel 9:7, where David says to Mephibosheth, "I will restore to you all the land that belonged to your grandfather Saul" (NIV).

However, the last phrase of Deuteronomy 4:9 deeply impacted me. Moses was reminding the elders of Israel of the works of God, and said, "Make them known to your children and your children's children" (ESV). About twelve years into my journey as a grandfather, I realized this passage gave me a mandate for my role in my family, and a purpose for the latter half of life: I was responsible to pass on God-stories to my grandchildren. This so powerfully spoke to me, that my wife and I moved from Illinois to southern California, so we could fulfill this command with our son's family, as his children were starting to grow up.

Then, Psalm 78:5b–6 told me how I was to *think* as a grandfather. Four generations are the subject of blessings and cursing in Scripture, but in this passage, it is in regard to passing on faith in the family: "he commanded *our fathers* [generation 1] to teach to *their children* [generation 2], that the next generation might know them, the *children yet unborn* [generation 3], and arise and tell them to *their children* [generation 4]" (ESV, emphasis added).

When I—generation 1—am teaching my children, I am to keep two generations not yet born in mind. My objective in my family is not to *pass on* faith, but to *perpetuate* faith. That means, as a grandfather, I am not only to have my grandchildren in view, but my grandchildren's *grandchildren.*

These two passages form the framework of responsibility for the grandparent role. Yet, many other Scriptures flesh out the duties and obligations of grandparents, either through examples or commands. For example, Jacob blessed Joseph's two boys in Genesis 48; grandparents are commanded to be God-storytellers in Exodus 10:2; Naomi is comforted by the birth of her grandson, Obed, in Ruth 4. Joshua set up the monument of stones to remind future generations

(Joshua 4). The Jews established the feast of Purim in Esther 9 and said it was to "never die out" (Esther 9:28, MSG).

### Themes Relating to Grandparenting

There are themes related to grandparenting (the numbers below vary some according to translation, but these are based upon the NIV). Throughout Scripture, we are urged (about 80 times) to remember God's character, words, and works, as well as our trials and failures and the faithfulness of those who have gone before us.

And why all the references—119 in all—to *generations*? Why is God the God of Abraham, Isaac, and Jacob? Because there is the expectation of the perpetuation of faith down through time. *Ancestors* appears 312 times, and a recurring theme in the Old Testament is, "learn from your ancestors"—either their failures or God's provision for them.

All of these, together with the over 200 references to *heritage* and *inheritance* provide a compelling foundation for a multi-generational view of family, church, and spiritual life.

## The Potential for Discipleship

Wayne Rice is one of the fathers of youth ministry in American churches: he was a co-founder of Youth Specialties, wrote over 30 books on youth ministry, and for over two decades, presented his "Understanding Your Teenager" seminar to thousands of parents all over the world. Currently, he is one of our staff members. When our ministry, Legacy Coalition, was still just an idea, I met with Wayne for lunch to talk about my passion for engaging grandparents. Afterward, I received an email from him that went something like this: "Larry, I just realized something. For many years, I started off 'Understanding Your Teenager' by showing the audience a 'pyramid of influence' illustration. In the pyramid, parents were at the top, then grandparents, then youth pastors and workers, then others, etc. My point was to emphasize to youth workers how important it was that they involve parents. *But every time I taught—for twenty years—I would emphasize parents and then skip over grandparents. I never once talked about them in my seminars.*"

Wayne's experience is not unique; while Christian grandparents have incredible potential as disciplers, that potential is unrecognized and under-resourced in the vast majority of churches. If you were to ask the leadership in your church to rank the various spiritual influencers of the children in your church according to their potential to disciple, what response do you think you would get? Hopefully, parents would be listed first, because they *are* influencers with the most potential, and, biblically, they are first responsible for the spiritual development of their children. But who would they list as second? A children's ministry worker? Youth pastor? The senior pastor?

## Grandparents Are Number Two

Children's ministry workers aren't second, because even children from church-going families aren't in attendance often enough. In my previous ministry as a children's ministry consultant, I found that in most megachurches, the average frequency of attending church was just over one time a month.[2] Youth pastors aren't second, because they don't typically stay in their position long enough for significant impact.

The simple truth is this: *grandparents* are number two when it comes to potential for spiritual impact. They, potentially, are ideal disciplers: they have a long-term relationship with their grandchildren. They *love* them. They *know* them already—their weaknesses and strengths, and their personalities. They're familiar with their

[2] Larry Fowler, *The Questions Nobody Asks About Our Children*, (Awana Clubs International, 2014), 17.

family situation. They have some wisdom to share. They are committed to their spiritual growth and will still be there when there are failures. All of these are desirable traits of a discipler, and grandparents perfectly fit the mold!

In reality, however, grandparents are often the number one spiritual influencers in the lives of their grandchildren, because parents aren't fulfilling their biblical responsibilities as they should. When parents don't prioritize spiritual instruction, are indifferent, or even worse, are opposed to it, grandparents are usually the primary spiritual influencers in a child's life.

## National Potential

There are an estimated 30 million Christian grandparents in the U.S. While estimates differ, various studies set the number of grandparents as between 70 and 80 million,[3] and other studies reveal that at least 40% of grandparent age groups profess to be born again.[4] Multiplying these numbers together results in the 30 million estimate. When their kids are done having children, they will have an average of six grandchildren.[5] While there is overlap (my wife and I both have seven grandchildren, but they are the same seven), my guesstimate is that 75 million or more of the youngest Americans have a Christian grandparent.

Christian grandparents also have many years of influence: the average age when a person becomes a grandparent in the U.S. is 50.[6] Most will spend one-third to one-half of their lives in this role. My wife, Diane, and I were married at 20; our daughter at 19, and we be-

---

[3] "The Grandparent Boom," AARP, https://www.aarp.org/home-family/friends-family/info-2017/record-number-grandparents.html.

[4] "Evangelicals in America: The Stats May Surprise You," The Gospel Coalition, https://www.thegospelcoalition.org/article/evangelicals-surprise/.

[5] "Demographic Information About Grandparents Today," Susan Adcox, https://www.liveabout.com/grandparents-demographic-information-1695746. 2019.

[6] AARP, "2018 Grandparents Today National Survey." https://doi.org/10.26419/res.00289.001.

came grandparents at 43. If my life expectancy as stated by the Social Security tables holds true, we will spend half of our lives as grandparents. I believe grandparents are the youngest they have ever been in the history of earth—not in age, but in health, energy, and vitality.

All of these numbers testify to the incredible potential for spiritual impact in the youngest generations by grandparents. Yet, most Christian grandparents are missing opportunities, because they simply haven't thought about their potential or haven't learned of the biblical mandates that can guide their role.

## The Dangers of the Cultural View

Tom didn't want to go to the conference. His wife, Nancy, on staff at a church, registered for our Legacy Grandparenting Conference—and she didn't want to go alone. Finally, Tom relented and went. But he admitted afterward that he couldn't imagine what he was going to learn, because—after all—he was a "good" grandparent.

In the early days of our ministry, I was setting up a display table at a ministry event, hoping to make some connections. A gray-haired man walked by, and I was in recruitment mode. I thought he might be a grandparent, so I tried to get his attention: "Excuse me, are you a grandparent?" He just kept walking. "No thanks," he said, brushing me off with a polite rejection, "I'm good." I knew he meant, "I've got it down as a grandparent; I don't need help."

Later, I learned his name was Richard. Today, he and Tom are both zealous advocates of being an *intentional* grandparent. They both listened to a new vision for their role and understood what Scripture said. Now they both have a new vision for their role as grandfathers and are much more effective in how they are fulfilling that role.

We all—Christian or not—want to be a "good" grandparent. And in a typical church, the majority of grandparents in the congregation, like Tom and Richard, see themselves as already good at what they do with their grandkids. However, most have never been asked, "By what standard are you a good grandparent? Is your standard your personal experience, cultural norms, or biblical truth?" Let's examine these more closely.

## The Standard of Personal Experience

Many grandparents, even Christian ones, compare themselves to their personal experience with their own grandparents. Recently, a speaker on our weekly webinar, Grand Monday Nights, related how three of his four grandparents had passed away, and the only one that he ever met was angry, judgmental, and demanding. He said he determined he was never going to be a grandfather like that.

A grandmother related to us how her grandfather, a pastor even, was gruff and cross with her and her siblings, and she, like the speaker, was resolved to be different. Others have had wonderful, influential grandparents, and they aspire to be like them. Many have had grandparents who were not engaged, not living close, or who had passed away. The wide variety of personal experiences means a different standard for being a "good" grandparent other than one's own family situation is needed.

## The Standard of Culture

The voice that instructs a majority of grandparents—even Christian ones—about what makes a good grandparent, is the cultural voice. Through the years, we are taught by conversations, pictures, news, and even jokes, what the "proper" way to grandparent is. I've heard the line "If I knew that grandkids were this much fun, I would have had them first" so many times, that it simply isn't funny to me anymore. The reality is, grandkids aren't always fun—especially when they get older, make wrong decisions, or just begin to pull away from a close relationship with us. But the influences of society lead us to believe that we are a good grandparent if we go to their soccer games, help take care of them, shower them with gifts, and spoil them a bunch.

We've all heard the phrase, "sugar them up and send them home." One can buy books on Amazon like *Grandpas Are for Finding Worms* and Gra*ndmas Are for Giving Tickles.* Those titles illustrate the notion that a grandparent's role is primarily to provide fun and companionship. My friend, Dr. Josh Mulvihill, author of several books on grandparenting, likes to summarize the cultural view of what makes a good grandparent with the words, "trusted playmate."[7]

The perception of a grandparent's role is further complicated by the pull from advertising, social pressure, and our materialistic society, to "retire and go play." There is a strong message of retirement narcissism: "You've earned it—go enjoy life while you can." The advertisements for retirement villages and ocean cruises present a picture of a carefree life full of enjoyment and romance: golf shots landing in the center of the green, carefree relaxation by the side of a pool, or couples enjoying a moonlit evening on the deck of a cruise ship. But indulgence in these retirement pleasures too often results in diminished time and relationships with family, and sometimes it causes resentment and bitterness because the grandparents are not available to the grandkids. You've probably seen the bumper sticker, "We're spending our kids' inheritance:" it is a clear statement of self-gratification over family investment, fueled by the message of culture about what retirement life is to be like.

But Scripture has a higher bar for us grandparents.

[7] Dr. Josh Mulvihill, *Biblical Grandparenting* (Bethany House Publishers, 2018), 133–134.

## The Standard of Biblical Truth

Christian grandparents love the Lord—and they love their grandchildren. They also want those precious grandkids to grow up loving God. Yet most have not considered the passages in Scripture that inform their role as grandparents.

I often ask grandparent audiences, "How many of you have ever heard a sermon, read a book, or attended a class on your role as a grandparent?" When our ministry was formed in 2016, our informal polling found that only about one percent responded in the positive to that question. My personal experience has continued to confirm that. At one grandparenting presentation with an audience of 250, I asked that question and only three raised their hands. In my most recent seminar, ALL of the attendees indicated it was the very first time they had ever received any instruction of any kind on their role.

A super-majority of Christian grandparents are simply uninformed about the biblical standard for their role as a grandparent or what to do to have spiritual influence. Some, however, have figured it out on their own. In his research, Dr. Mulvihill found that while all Christian grandparents said the spiritual development of grandchildren was important to them, only one in four were actually doing something about it.[8]

In our Legacy Coalition seminars, webinars, and conferences, we have found grandparents to be eager to have a greater spiritual influence—to seek to meet that higher bar the Bible portrays for them. They want to meet the scriptural standard—but they need awakening, encouragement, and equipping. When a local church addresses their role, it is a blessing to the grandparents for sure, but it's also a benefit to that congregation.

[8] Mulvihill, *Biblical Grandparenting*, 143.

## The Benefit to a Church

"We've got to reach young families!" If that's not the passion of a pastor, it should be. One of the saddest sights in churches (I've seen it myself) is to stand in the back of a service and see that all the heads of the congregation are gray or bald. One pastor, who had that kind of a congregation, expressed it to me this way: "I'm just trying to keep us out of the casket." It has distressed me, however, to see that too often the effort to reach young families has the unintended result of marginalizing those who are older. One large megachurch that I attended for a few years had all younger leadership—only one person was over 45. Many of my peers, while they appreciated the many young people who were coming to Christ through the church, felt they weren't wanted or needed—except for their tithe, or to serve as greeters or parking lot attendants. Before long, we all moved to other churches where there was a greater opportunity to serve.

**JJ:** *I led the student ministry at our church a few years ago in an interim position to bring both campuses together in collaboration and to help them begin thinking toward a more intentional family ministry focus and to mentor the new central youth pastor. During that time, I encouraged the team to begin to think about recruiting older volunteers, specifically those who were grandparents. Until this time, recruiting youth workers was limited to college and former students who attended. They were missing a key volunteer pool with much more capacity. Now, there are some grandparents who lead in the student ministry. As I think back through my years in student and family ministry, there are a handful of key older adults who were some of my best youth workers. At a former church, one is still leading eighth grade girls and has influenced hundreds of young ladies in that ministry, including my own daughter. That legacy of faith is priceless!*

That sentiment, "We've got to reach young families" is a response I've gotten over and over again as we've presented our ministry to church leaders. They were telling me that they just didn't see grandparents as a priority. I've always been patient with such a response because I knew that what I was presenting was a paradigm shift. I would respond, "So do we!" A grandparent ministry is ALL about reaching the youngest generations for Christ, and it is an effective, energizing way to engage the older third of the congregation in that mission.

## Grandparenting Is Not Senior Adult Ministry

Let me repeat some of my earlier points that contrast a senior adult ministry with a grandparenting ministry:

- Senior adult ministry has to do with an age group, while grandparenting ministry has to do with a family relationship.
- Senior adult ministries are mostly about ministering *to* seniors (inward-focused); grandparenting ministry is about *equipping* grandparents for ministry (outward-focused).
- Senior adult ministry usually has a prescribed format—a traditional service, fellowship outings, and "helping" projects like folding bulletins. A grandparenting ministry simply fits into the DNA of the church; for example, if yours is a small-group-oriented church, then small groups who have grandparents in them focus from time to time on getting equipped and encouraged in their role.

## Reducing Crankiness

A grandparenting vision can transform the attitude of those who are older. A few years ago, a grandmother approached me at a break in the seminar I was leading. She appeared to be in her mid-80s and spoke with a frail voice. With no introduction, she began: "Mr. Fowler, I want to tell you a story. I *hate* the music in my church (yes, she emphasized the word hate). It is so loud—I just sit and tolerate it until it is time for the sermon. Then one weekend, my 19-year-old grandson came to visit me, and agreed to go with me to church. That Sunday, I found myself sitting there, desperately hoping that my grandson would like the music." And with that, she turned and walked away.

What she was relating to me was profound: she was telling me that her love and concern for her grandson made her attitude about the music in the service do a 180-degree pivot. We've seen many, many grandparents do that about-face when their church embraces their love and concern for their grandchildren. I believe, when we align what we do with their love for their grandchildren, they are much more positive about the larger church efforts to reach and engage younger generations.

## Ministering to the Greatest Heart-Pains

We've also found that many grandparents are masking some of the greatest heart-pains of life when they come to church. While prayer requests for physical ailments and conditions increase as they get older to the point that a prayer time in a class or small group becomes somewhat of an "organ recital," the deepest aches in their soul are kept hidden. Those have to do with adult children who have walked away from faith, broken relationships, and bad decisions by family members. When the church begins to address those greatest heart-pains, giving hope and equipping them with new strategies, grandparents are endeared to the church and energized for impact in their family.

As an older adult, I say often, "There is nothing I want more than to see my grandkids in Heaven with me." And I follow by that by quoting my own version of 3 John 4:4, "I have no greater joy than to hear that my [grand]children are walking in the truth" (ESV, emphasis added). So many Christian grandparents echo my sentiment. And when a church recognizes that desire and then encourages and equips them to impact their grandchildren, they are aligned with a broader church vision to reach young people for Christ.

## What God Is Doing

There is now a growing global movement of intentional Christian grandparents. While still in its infancy, the growth is something that only God could make happen. Our own ministry, Legacy Coalition, has nearly doubled every year since we began. We have seen tens of thousands of grandparents rise up and eagerly begin to be intentional about spiritually influencing the youngest generations in their family.

And churches are catching the vision: in 2016, we were not able to find a single church in America that was attempting to equip grandparents on even a semi-regular basis. In 2025, over 2,500 churches now see the value of grandparents and are resourcing them through classes, small groups, seminars, sermons, and more.

Christian camps are holding grandparent-grandchild events, or multi-generational family camps. We are not aware of a single grandparenting ministry or resource in any other country ten years ago—now there are burgeoning ministries in a number, and interest from many more. At the time of this writing, Camp Caraway and Truett Conference Center in North Carolina, Twin Lakes Bible Camp in Iowa, and Mount Hermon Christian Conference Center in California are examples of camps that provide these opportunities.

Christian schools—elementary, secondary, and even higher education institutions—are beginning to include equipping and inspiration as part of how they connect with grandparents.

Ten years ago, there was not a single grandparenting ministry or resource in existence in any other country that we are aware of—now there are burgeoning ministries in eight, and interest from many more.

## What About Grandparents Raising Grandchildren?

"There are a lot of grandparents raising grandkids these days, aren't there?" That question is often posed first when I bring up the subject of grandparenting, especially to people in leadership positions—because that is what they have heard about. "Yes, there are," my answer starts. "But the truth is, they don't get to be grandparents, because they are completely occupied with being parents." The numbers are staggering—in the U.S. alone, 2.07 million grandparents are raising their grandchildren.[9]

Do you have them in your church? Likely, yes. Do you know who they are? Likely, no. Grandparents raising grandchildren (often referred to as GRGs) may be those in the most need of support from the local church. In his book, *Raising Your Grandchildren*, Cavin Harper gives a plea to pastors:

> There is likely a significant and growing demographic in your congregation about which you may have little knowledge. While there have always been grandparents who are raising their grandchildren, never have we faced a growing epidemic like is occurring today. And never has this segment of the body of Christ been so invisible to us.[10]

---

[9] "Grandchildren Being Raised by Grandparents," Department of Labor, https://www.dol.gov/agencies/wb/topics/grandparents-raising-grandkids, (2021).

[10] Cavin Harper, *Raising Your Grandchildren* (Bethany House Publishers, 2020), 97.

## The Invisible Grandparents

Because their situation was born out of a family trauma, they often have no support system. A single mother might have her mom, a sister, or someone else to help, but grandparents raising grandchildren often have no one else. However, they can be invisible to the church leadership. Consider these factors that cause them to stay in the background:

- *They are tired.* One of my friends is fond of saying about grandkids, "We are so excited to see the headlights when the grandchildren come to visit, but we are just as excited to see the taillights when they leave." His point? Grandkids wear grandparents out, even when they visit for a couple of days. *GRGs never see those taillights.* When grandparents have full custody, they often don't have the energy to do much more in the local church than bring those grandkids to one service a week.
- *They don't fit.* When the children's ministry has a parent meeting or event, grandparents are very aware of the age difference between them and the rest of the group. They also don't fit with their age group because everyone else is free of the responsibility of raising children and they are not. In either case, they choose not to attend—it's just easier.
- *Many are embarrassed.* The mere fact that they have custody of their grandchildren means there has been a traumatic event in their family. Sometimes it is a tragedy, like the death of a parent—but more often, it is because the parent is addicted to drugs, incarcerated, or mentally ill. They prefer not to share those details with the church body, so they just stay quiet and out of sight.

**RG:** *These are great insights and truly need to be considered! As Larry points out, grandparents do not have the energy they once had raising their own children. One of the best things a church can do is to partner these grandchildren up with younger and more energetic mentors. This is another way to achieve more intentional intergenerational ministry! If the term "mentoring" scares folks, the fact is we are just encouraging others to provide "Christian nurture" for these children.*

## What Can a Church Do?

1. Begin by identifying them personally. A bulletin announcement probably won't do it. Watching for grandparents bringing grandchildren to children's and youth ministry and engaging them in a conversation on an individual basis is best.
2. Then, learn their situation—they are all so different. Here are a few that are I know of:
   - A 70-year-old grandma has custody of her five-year-old granddaughter; her husband has Alzheimer's, so she can't leave the granddaughter with him even to go get groceries. She has a friend who sometimes helps, but she desperately needs a babysitter.
   - A 72-year-old couple have adopted their two *great*-grandchildren, ages 2 and 5. Along with that commitment, I'm sure they prayed that they would live to at least 90. They need someone to help them have a break!
   - A single grandma has custody of 14-year-old triplets. One is autistic; all three are a handful in terms of discipline, attitude, and achievement in school. She needs additional positive mentors in their lives.

- A grandparent couple have custody of four grandchildren, ages 8 to 13. The grandma has MS and must be wheeled in a wheelchair; the grandpa has his own health issues and walks with a cane. They need compassion and help!

3. Institute a "church grandpa and grandma" effort. Recruit grandparents who don't have any grandchildren living locally to come beside these very needy peers and be the grandparents that the GRGs aren't able to be. What do they do to help? What a biological grandparent would do: love, support, pray.

## How to Begin a Grandparenting Ministry

As churches have embraced the vision of the importance of grandparenting, they have begun to address the role in various ways, depending on size, culture, age demographics, and other factors. Yet, there are steps that are common to most that can guide the establishment of a grandparenting ministry.

Step 1—Pastoral Support: lay people who feel called to start this ministry in their church must secure the buy-in of a pastor who recognizes the importance of intentional Christian grandparenting and will encourage their efforts. The greater the pastoral ownership, the greater the chance of success in establishing the ministry.

Step 2—Prayer Team: developing a prayer team of interested grandparents is absolutely essential to establishing a spiritual foundation for the ministry. The prayer team would focus first on praying for openness in the hearts of the grandparents in the church, and wisdom in how to launch the ministry.

Step 3—Introduce Intentional Christian Grandparenting: generate interest through a live presentation. This may be a sermon, a luncheon, after-church meeting, announcement in the worship service, or a resource table in the foyer. The more exposure the better, of course, and the greater the engagement of the senior pastor in casting this vision, the greater the chance of a good launch. If they are needed, Legacy Coalition has lots of resources that can help with the content for such a vision-casting event: videos, books, and blogs.

Step 4—Visionary/Equipping Study: schedule and promote an initial Grandparenting Matters study. Depending on your particular church, this may be organized as a 6 to 12-week video small-group study in a Sunday School class or small group, or a live seminar by Legacy staff. The Grandparenting Matters curriculum was created to be "Christian grandparenting 101," and should be the first step in envisioning and equipping grandparents.

Step 5—Core Team: planning and support: out of the first group of grandparents to go through the Grandparenting Matters study, identify and establish a team of passionate volunteers that will be committed to serve as the driving force to launch and sustain a grandparenting ministry. They are responsible for scheduling and implementing the ministry plan and coordinating with the church staff.

The following three steps are not sequential but will be determined by how you develop your ministry plan; in fact, they will likely be key elements in your plan.

Step 6a—Paradigm Shift: include the grandparenting role when you do "family" things. In his sermons, your pastor can say "parents and grandparents" instead of just "parents." Include grandparents in baby dedications. Get them up on the stage behind the parents and give a challenge to them as well. Have a grandparent event in your children's and youth ministries, just like you do for parents.

Step 6b—Equipping Events: each church will identify what the ministry looks like on an ongoing basis. It may include focusing on grandparenting in classes or small groups from time to time, periodic grandparenting events, hosting the Legacy Grandparenting Summit, service events, prayer groups, etc.

Step 6c—Service Events: re-engage grandparents in children's and youth ministries in ways that fit their life situation. You can have them volunteer once a month in children's ministry, provide refreshments at a youth event, have a "serve day" where grandparents and grandkids work as teams; have them pair up with a teenager in the youth group to pray for that teen, etc.

## Conclusion

I urge you—*join this movement.* Begin envisioning and equipping the grandparents in your church. It will give new vision to the grandparents in your congregation. It will provide hope for those who are hurting. It will align them with your church's mission to disciple younger generations. It will lead to the salvation of many grandchildren—and generations beyond. It could change your church—and it could change our country.

*Start now.* Grandparents are acutely aware of how quickly life goes by, and their window of influence will close rapidly. Leveraging their potential for spiritual impact in the youngest generations is an urgent endeavor.

May God greatly lead you and "grandly" bless your efforts!

**References**

AARP. "*The Grandparent Boom.*" https://www.aarp.org/home-family/friends-family/info-2017/record-number-grandparents.html.

AARP. "2018 Grandparents Today National Survey." https://www.aarp.org/content/dam/aarp/research/surveys_statistics/life-leisure/2019/aarp-grandparenting-study.doi.10.26419-2Fres.00289.001.pdf.

Adcox, Susan. *Demographic Information About Grandparents Today.* https://www.liveabout.com/grandparents-demographic-information-1695746. 2019.

Department of Labor. (2021). "Grandchildren Being Raised by Grandparents." https://www.dol.gov/agencies/wb/topics/grandparents-raising-grandkids.

Fowler, Larry. *The Question Nobody Asks About Our Children.* Awana Clubs International, 2014.

Harper, Cavin. *Raising Your Grandchildren.* Bethany House Publishers, 2020.

Mulvihill, Dr. Josh. (2018). *Biblical Grandparenting.* Bethany House Publishers, 2018.

The Gospel Coalition. (2021). "Evangelicals in America: The Stats May Surprise You." https://www.thegospelcoalition.org/article/evangelicals-surprise/.

## Chapter 4

# Engaging and Equipping Foster and Adoptive Families

Rich Griffith, D.Min.

I had gotten to know Sherry (not her real name) when I was assisting a church's youth ministry. Sherry checked many of the boxes this book discusses. She is a widow, a single grandparent who is parenting her adopted granddaughter. Sherry's husband had passed away several years ago and her daughter was unable to care for Sherry's granddaughter. Sherry did the right thing by pursuing kinship adoption of her granddaughter. As adoptive single parents, we had a lot in common. Sherry was just one of many others who have told me they feel like a fifth wheel at church. Sherry's comment was a bit shocking to me, but the more I evaluated her comment I had to agree: "Pastor Rich, the church has made an idol out of marriage."

I cannot begin to tell you how many times people have tried to "set me up" on dates as the predominant view in our culture is that all pastors should be married. In fact, I was recently considered for an interview on a very well-known national radio show. The interview was going to cover my first book, *Voices: Helping Children and Youth Listen to Wise Counsel.* Everything was going well in the vetting process and subsequent conversations that took place. There seemed to be some genuine excitement about the interview. The excitement waned when members of the vetting team discovered I was a single, unmarried dad with adopted children.

What was most painful about the situation was not that I would not be on the radio, rather it was the pain in feeling that I did not measure up. Of course, if you are a parent, you know this feeling all too well. If you are a single parent, you know this feeling even more. The issue was not the content of the book, rather the potential rejection I felt because I am a dad of a "non-traditional" family. It was for biblical reasons that I came to have my own children as I was on a journey of living out James 1:27 which states, "Religion that God our Father accepts as pure and faultless is this: to look after orphans and widows in their distress and to keep oneself from being polluted by the world" (NIV). (The good news is after some theological explanation of my situation the radio program decided to host me after all.)

My colleague, Dr. Chris Shirley in his book, *Family Ministry and the Church* under a section entitled, "Prepare for diverse ministry," writes:

> Teach the ideal, but minister to the reality. Every family in your church, regardless of their composition, deserves respect, attention, care, and recognition within the larger strategy for ministry to, with, and through families. Most family ministry models are designed around the traditional and intact model. Focus on a biblical model for family (in light of the reality within your church) that acknowledges the various family structures in your church.[1]

What great insight! This consideration is what we mean when we begin to discuss defining family beyond culture and biology—we are defining family *theologically*. We must do so because everyone's family journey is different. This is certainly true of my family journey.

---

[1] Chris Shirley, *Family Ministry and the Church* (Randall House Publishing, 2018).

I vividly remember the call to adopt. I was reading through the book of James and James 1:27 hit me like a ton of bricks, smashing my "safe" world to pieces. For four years I wrestled with fear that kept me from adopting—especially as a single man. I remember praying, "Lord, it just doesn't *look* right … a single man in youth ministry adopting? People are going to (and probably still do) think I am weird!" I felt what Hosea must have felt when being told by God to marry Gomer, a prostitute. How can a faithful man of God be given such a seemingly contradictory command? Of course, we know that God called Hosea to do this to model God's faithful response to an unfaithful Israel. I was being called to be a faithful dad to young men who had none.

Needless to say, the call to adopt felt way out of place. I was single, traveling the world, consulting and thoroughly enjoying my own little world. However, after reading James 1:27, I had a four year "Jonah" experience of running from God. After multiple God-orchestrated circumstances and conversations that are too long for this book, I could no longer run. After doing more research, I was compelled to adopt older kids since children over the age of eight have a greater risk of "aging out of the system" and face significant societal marginalization. There is a plethora of research that shows 50% of children who age-out of the system lose much needed support systems, wind up homeless, incarcerated, sex-trafficked, or dead. Many children, who are in foster care and reach the age of eight (second grade), will age out of the system. Other horrific things happen as well. For example, 60% of young women who age out of the system end up in the sex industry. This is unacceptable!

As a pastor and dad with fourteen years of foster and adoption experience with three adopted sons, I have a unique perspective on feeling like a "fifth wheel" in the life of the church—especially when it comes to youth and family ministries. Keep in mind, I felt like a fifth wheel even as I was serving on staff! The sentiment of feeling like a fifth wheel at church has been already expressed by many of the contributing authors to this book. This is another reason we *must* consider a theological definition of *family*. If we fail to define families theologically, many godly Christians, who are trying to follow the will of God (Matthew 12:46–50), will continue to feel left out. Our families will continue to feel isolated from the family of God and the life of the church.

> **JJ:** *Rich gets to the heart of the issue. Jesus intended His Church to corporately act as a family system—an eternal family that supersedes all others. Our theology informs our praxis. In other words: what we* believe *determines what we* do. *If we indeed believe that the local church is to express our adoption in Christ as brothers and sisters, then this conviction will permeate every program, ministry, and teaching. A biblical model of family included everyone, and all have a seat at the table.*

Being a parent has been, and continues to be, one of the most emotion-laden experiences of my life. If you are a parent, you know what I am talking about. Being a single adoptive parent carries a good number of additional challenges. I seriously thought I would lose my ministry and my job due to the number of times I was called to my sons' school. The trauma foster children experience often leads to them having significant emotional and behavior issues. Being a single parent means you are the only parent that can go get your children from school when trauma-triggered incidences happen. As schools are challenged to deal with kids with trauma, behavioral issues mean you may have to take your children with you into your workplace or miss work. Public schools are not well-equipped to deal with kids from difficult backgrounds. This is a daunting thought considering that our children and youth are experiencing more significant societal traumas.

**SM:** *Many churches are also not equipped to deal with kids from difficult backgrounds. Sometimes volunteers don't know the children and teens well enough to understand why certain things are triggering. Kids with trauma may struggle with the loud environments we have in children's ministry, the inconsistencies in routine, and the inconsistent volunteer structures we have in place. Any of those things can be difficult for kids with trauma because they are always on high alert, scanning their environment to make sure they are safe. Instead of trying to understand them, we sometimes make assumptions about their behavior that aren't always grace-based. One suggestion would be for churches to ask a parent of a child from a difficult background to observe the environment on Sunday morning. Ask them what things might be difficult for a child with a background of trauma. You might be surprised how insightful they are to you in thinking about ministry to kids from hard places.*

While all children who come out of hard places need support systems such as counseling and respite care, so do the families that take these children in. Frankly, when it came to becoming a dad, I cannot tell you the number of times I wanted to quit and say, "I can't do this! Us becoming a family is not working!" There were times I did not feel like my sons and I were bonding. If the churches I served in did not treat my sons and I "as family" when they did, I would have given up. Unfortunately, understanding and compassionate church members and leadership are not always the case. There were times I was afraid of losing my ministry. As ministry leaders, we are always thinking about 1 Timothy 3:5 which says, "If anyone does not know how to manage his own family, how can he take care of God's church?" (NIV). It's challenging enough to wonder if you are a good enough parent, but it is another thing when you worry about what the rest of the church and your leadership thinks. Many times, I wished folks would understand the effects of trauma on a child, walk up to me and my sons, put an arm around us and just say, "We understand. This is hard, but we love you and we are praying for you! You are doing the best you can right now!"

My adoption journey began the process of understanding a theological framing of family. What Dr. Chap Clark has called, "adoptive church," JJ and I have called "church as family." Dr. Clark states it this way, "In the adoptive church we don't 'adopt' each other; rather, we recognize that each of us, in Christ, had been adopted by God.… The goal of adoptive ministry is that everything we think, do, and plan should enhance those familial relationships."[2]

## The Need

For the last several years, the number of children in foster care has ranged from a high 300 thousand to mid-500 thousand. If these children had a physical illness, it would be considered an epidemic. The only problem is that the epidemic of the number of children going into foster care never goes away. No doubt, taking in children who come from difficult and traumatic environments is an incredible challenge. As a single dad of three adopted sons who came out of the system, I know these challenges firsthand. Think about the number of orphans and fostered children in the Bible! One of the greatest prophets of Israel, Moses, was a foster child due to societal upheaval. The birth of Jesus Himself was not the traditional model. Born to a very young mother and cared for by Joseph, Jesus' birth was rather scandalous in a culture that valued lineage, tribes, and tight-knit families where the household had a strong male father figure and a nurturing mother. Society sure has changed, and these changes make

[2] Chap Clark, *Adoptive Church: Creating an Environment Where Emerging Generations Belong* (Baker Academic, 2018), 8.

parenting even more of a challenge. I will state this several times because it is important: you may not be called to foster or adopt, but all of us are called to minister to each other as the family of God.

## A Theology and History of Adoption

Adoption is nothing new to societies, theology, or the church. Jack Miles convincingly argues that a theology of adoption in the biblical narrative is a concept developed over time.[3] The title "children of God" became a progressive title, first among the people of Israel and then among individuals who chose to follow God. While ancient people may have practiced both formal and informal adoption-like transactions, the God of the Hebrew and Christian Scriptures gives us a theological model of adoption by allowing those who accept Jesus Christ as Savior to become the children of God. Humanity comes to be God's children *not* through a "natural birth process" but rather through a spiritual process of adoption, as stated in John 1:12–13: "Yet to all who did receive him, to those who believed in his name, he gave the right to become children of God—children born not of natural descent, nor of human decision or a husband's will, but born of God." John also wrote of being born again in John 3:3.

Moreover, human beings are "adopted" by God as His children at a point in time of their greatest need. Romans 5:8 shows God's love for humanity by stating, "But God demonstrates his own love for us in this: While we were still sinners, Christ died for us." This so speaks to the heart of fostering and adoption. During times of trauma, there are brave souls from all walks of life that step up and provide much-needed nurture—even as the child might initially reject that nurture. All children need physical care as well as spiritual and emotional nurture. Without elements of care and nurture, children

[3] Jack Miles, "Israel as Foundling: Abandonment, Adoption, and the Fatherhood of God." *Hebrew Studies* 46 (2005): 7–24.

face a traumatic and uncertain future. Let me reiterate this from personal experience: foster and adoptive parents cannot do this alone! Each community might have a foster parent support system, but they are not necessarily faith based. Since this is the case, it is important for foster and adoptive parents to find that support in their own local church family!

It would be good for us to remember when Jesus chastised His disciples as they prevented children from coming to Him to be blessed. Jesus said, "Let the little children come to me, and do not hinder them, for the kingdom of God belongs to such as these" (Luke 18:16b, NIV). Where a culture fails to see the intrinsic value of children among them, Jesus is sure to chastise that unwelcoming culture and welcome children by blessing them. John Wall states it well when he says, "The gospel emphasis on Jesus' nativity and its including children as first in the kingdom of God are taken to their logical conclusion, namely that children are the surest signs and representatives of God in this world."[4]

Vulnerable children without families are at risk of all types of horrors. I previously mentioned what happens when aging out of the system, but this pattern of being at risk starts early when our young people lack the support systems they need to navigate life. Children and youth who do not have their needs met are susceptible to systemic abandonment. Systemic abandonment is already happening in our culture with children and youth that come from intact, two-parent homes. It is worth repeating, systemic abandonment is when the institutions that are supposed to be about the well-being and nurture of children and youth become hijacked by adult-driven agendas. Systemic abandonment has become a reality in the lives of so many children and youth. Since it is not in the scope of this book, I refer you to any of the works of Dr. David Elkind or Dr. Chap Clark.

[4] John Wall, "Fallen Angels: A Contemporary Christian Ethical Ontology of Childhood," *International Journal of Practical Theology* 8, no. 2 (October 2004): 160–184.

Imagine the challenges of systemic abandonment for children who do not come from a background of two, loving, educated parents who will advocate for them! Theologically, members of the body of Christ are called to counter systemic abandonment and criminalization of the young by blessing and recognizing them as gifts from God (Psalm 127:3). I think it is important to consider *all children* as a gift from God—not just biological children. When children are among the church, believers are in the presence of the kingdom of God. Since Jesus and the Father are one (John 10:30), when Jesus blesses children and takes them into His arms, they are shown the heart of a nurturing and caring Father. Churches are called to emulate this behavior.

During the time of the early church, the apostle James encouraged the church to

look after orphans and widows. As a reminder, James 1:27 states, "Religion that God our Father accepts as pure and faultless is this: to look after orphans and widows in their distress and to keep oneself from being polluted by the world (NIV)." Even the harsh pagan world had a practice of taking orphans in. Considering this fact, the church should be even more compelled to take in those who are at risk of being abandoned and exploited because God the Father commands believers to take care of the vulnerable. The widows and orphans of James' day had the same needs as children and widows in ancient times. To be an orphan means someone who is "cast out," and a widow is someone who is vulnerable; both are often unable to provide for themselves, and both are at the mercy of society since they do not live under the legal protection of a family. The need for the church to meet the needs of the most vulnerable in a society has not changed (James 1:27; Isaiah 1:17).

**JJ:** *We see this throughout the early church. In 1 Timothy 5:1–8, Paul gave clear instructions rooted in this idea of family. Writing* *to Timothy leading the church in Ephesus—a culture of self-interest and paganism—Paul called believers to embody true spiritual community by caring for one another, especially those most often overlooked. In verse 4, Paul reminded believers that caring for aging or vulnerable family members is a practical act of worship. When biological family is absent or unable, the church steps in—not out of duty, but as an act of love.*

*This kind of worship is deeply relational and profoundly spiritual. It is how the church ministers to every kind of family, in every kind of situation. Paul's teaching is clear: the church should not allow anyone to slip through the cracks.*

There are an increasing number of churches who are engaging in adoption, and this is a wonderful reality. However, there is another reality where most churches are not very good at encouraging and equipping foster and adoptive families post-placement. Few churches (there are some) know how to support adoptive families after adoption has occurred. Supporting an adoption movement within a church has to be more than just encouraging your members to adopt. There must be support systems in place that will help spiritually nurture these families. Near the end of this chapter, I offer some insights on how some churches have provided support to foster and adoptive families. As mentioned, not everyone in the church is called to adopt, however everyone is called to care for "orphans and widows." The expectation to care for the marginalized is not just for families who adopt children. The expectation is for the church to become an adoptive family that walks through life with the adoptive parents and children. When a baby comes into a family, most churches are good about celebrating the new addition to the family. Infant baptisms and dedications typically involve some type of covenant agreement stating the church members will help spiritually nurture these families and children. Can I offer an honest observation? If we were truly taking these covenants of spiritual nurture seriously, why are so many of our young people leaving the church? If we are not going to "family each other," the promises we make to spiritually nurture our young are just empty ceremonies and words that bear little fruit.

## Biblical Support of Adoption

### Romans 8:14-17

When children are embraced into the life of a family, they are given a sense of identity and belonging. When God embraces human beings, they are given the message that they belong to Him, and it is in Him where they can find their identity. "The dual proclamation of Jesus Christ as God's son and of his disciples as sons or children of God was undoubtedly part of the early Christian kerygma.... It neatly encapsulated the vision of a familial bond under the headship of one heavenly Father."[5] Believers share a title with Christ: child(ren) of God. With God as our Father and having been adopted into the family of Christ, believers are called to emulate the action of adoption by bringing others into the family of God. Romans 8:14–17 reads:

> For those who are led by the Spirit of God are the children of God. The Spirit you received does not make you slaves, so that you live in fear again; rather, the Spirit you received brought about your adoption to sonship. And by him we cry, "*Abba*, Father." The Spirit himself testifies with our spirit that we are God's children. Now if we are children, then we are heirs—heirs of God and co-heirs with

[5] Michael Peppard, "Adopted and Begotten Sons of God: Paul and John on Divine Sonship," *The Catholic Biblical Quarterly* 73, no. 1 (January 2011): 92.

> Christ, if indeed we share in his sufferings in order that we may also share in his glory (NIV).

When children and youth experience challenging backgrounds and are at risk of being criminalized, thereby making them susceptible to incarceration, that is another form of slavery. When children are adopted into a family, whether literally or figuratively, into the life of a church, they can be nurtured in a way that helps them avoid the process of criminalization by giving them the support they need. That support may come in the way of advocacy, material provision, or mentoring. These are the types of actions that are a part of nurturing a child. Christians are called to provide the nurturing of children and youth, and it is nurture that keeps a child from the "slavery" of a penal institution. Theologically, when we are redeemed as God's children, we are nurtured into a life that releases us from the bondage of sin (Romans 6:6, NIV).

George C. Gianoulis states, "The sonship of believers is an important theme in Romans 8. Paul used the honorific title *υίοι θεού* twice [son of God] (verses 14, 19), *τέκνα θεοί* [child of God] three times (verses 16, 17, 21), and *υιοθεσία* [adoption as sons] twice (verses 15, 23). These terms all define the status of believers before God, that is, those who have new life in the Spirit."[6] If there is any segment of a society's population that needs a sense of a "new life," certainly those who are in foster care, without a family and in need of mentoring and nurture, fit the bill. Supporting foster families by mentoring their foster children brings much needed support to both the children and the adults attempting to heal wounded spirits. Furthermore, *spiritual adoption through mentoring by church members can help foster and adoptive children avoid being enslaved to a system where the odds are stacked against them.* Spiritual mentoring of foster and adoptive children can re-paint a picture of God's faithfulness to

[6] George C. Gianoulis, "Is Sonship in Romans 8:14–17 a Link with Romans 9?" *Bibliotheca Sacra* 166, no. 661 (January 2009): 70–83.

them. In other words, seeing at-risk children as "our children" brings with it an opportunity at a new life that might not have been possible without intentional mentoring and nurture. Every child that comes from a challenging background needs the opportunity for a new life.

While their biological family may have abandoned them, God's Church—that is,

the body of Christ—can show foster and adopted children they will not abandon them. When children are adopted through spiritual mentoring, they are no longer abandoned. Churches can remind children of the comfort Jesus gave all believers, that He would never "leave" or forsake us (John 14:18). Their futures are redeemed (Galatians 3:14). With redeemed futures comes the promise of being heirs in the kingdom of God (Romans 8:17). Since God adopted believers, and our adoption was made possible by sharing in the suffering of Christ, we as a church can help a child carry his or her burdens while mentoring that child. When Christ-followers mentor a youth or child through spiritual adoption, they can develop an understanding of their suffering. Hope for a child comes when, through mentoring, believers share in the glory of healing the heart and life of a child who might have continued in a life of rejection, fear, and criminalization.

## Galatians 4:1-7

When a child experiences both legal and spiritual adoption, a whole new world of opportunities opens to that child. Resources that were at one time either unavailable or fleeting are now available. The allocation of resources changes the future of the child, youth, or family that has experienced spiritual adoption. In Galatians 4:1–7, the apostle Paul wrote:

> What I am saying is that as long as an heir is underage, he is no different from a slave, although he owns the whole estate. The heir is subject to

> guardians and trustees until the time set by his father. So also, when we were underage, we were in slavery under the elemental spiritual forces of the world. But when the set time had fully come, God sent his Son, born of a woman, born under the law, to redeem those under the law, that we might receive adoption to sonship. Because you are his sons, God sent the Spirit of his Son into our hearts, the Spirit who calls out, "*Abba*, Father." So you are no longer a slave, but God's child; and since you are his child, God has made you also an heir (NIV).

Like Romans 8:14–17, the passage above highlights redemption, sonship, *Abba*, Father, slavery, and heirs. In Galatians 4:1–7, Paul used the imagery of slavery, children, and redemption to point out how those under the shackles of slavery have little control over their social, financial, personal, and current circumstances. Especially vulnerable to a system of slavery and abuse are those children who come from fractured families or who have no family at all.

Today, just as in Paul's day, those who lack family connections and resources are vulnerable to the abuses of an unjust society. Even if children are more empowered with social capital, every child needs a guardian or mentor to help them understand how to best function and use that empowerment. Understanding and wisdom can only be passed on through nurturing relationships with adults who partner with parents and guardians. Parents, as well as guardians, who have participated in the spiritual adoption of children must advocate for children. They must also help children live into the new life and freedom they have now been given.

Helping children understand that they have been freed from the past is especially true for at-risk children. It may be difficult for them to understand they have been removed from the "spiritual forces in the world" that have oppressed them. Much of the terminology Paul used here in Galatians 4:1–5 seems to come from an understanding of Greco-Roman laws and language.[7] In other words, Greco-Roman laws recognized the validity of sonship, inheritance, and guardianship and how family structures were impacted. Churches that have infant and child baptisms and dedications mirror Greco-Roman understanding of guardian responsibility in a spiritual way. In churches that practice any sort of covenant agreement with parents pertaining to spiritually raising children, an understanding of Galatians 4:1–7 shows a spiritual obligation to treat *all* children as heirs in their congregation. The obligation of spiritual nurture understands that the call to nurture does not matter whether the family is biological, foster, or adoptive.

Ephesians 1:2–10

For children coming from difficult backgrounds, forgiveness, redemption, and a sense of belonging are essential elements of healthy development. Spiritual adoption allows the church to teach all youth and children what it means to live a spiritual life where they experience these essential elements. Moreover, in a mentoring relationship, either the mentor or the mentee initiates the relationship by choosing the other. Ephesians 1:2–10 describes what it means to be chosen spiritually and how being chosen impacts relationships. Ephesians 1:2–10 states:

> Grace and peace to you from God our Father and the Lord Jesus Christ. Praise be to the God and Father of our Lord Jesus Christ, who has blessed us in the heavenly realms with every spiritual blessing in Christ. For he chose us in him before the creation of the world to be holy and blameless in his sight. In love he predestined us for adoption

[7] John K. Goodrich, "'As Long as the Heir Is a Child': The Rhetoric of Inheritance in Galatians 4:1–2 and P. Ryl. 2.153," *Novum Testamentum* 55, no. 1 (2013): 61–76.

> to sonship through Jesus Christ, in accordance with his pleasure and will—to the praise of his glorious grace, which he has freely given us in the One he loves. In him we have redemption through his blood, the forgiveness of sins, in accordance with the riches of God's grace that he lavished on us. With all wisdom and understanding, he made known to us the mystery of his will according to his good pleasure, which he purposed in Christ, to be put into effect when the times reach their fulfillment—to bring unity to all things in heaven and on earth under Christ (NIV).

When youth and children are mentored, they can begin to understand the love Christ has for them as shown through the body of Christ. Foster care, adoption, and mentoring hold much in common with the theology shown. Of most importance is the concept of election as found in Ephesians 1:2–10—that is, the concept of being chosen blameless in Christ. Christian theology emphasizes forgiveness, redemption, and being chosen and loved as a child of God.

In all aspects of mentoring and adoption, part of gaining an inheritance is an act of receiving empowerment through what parents have accumulated and passed on to their heirs. Once again, it does not matter whether the parent is a spiritual or physical parent. Spiritual mentoring mirrors adoption and the adopted receive an inheritance of a new life, both temporal and potentially eternal. With a plethora of Scripture that teaches what it means to be children of God (Matthew 5:9; Mark 10:14; Luke 20:36; John 1:12; Romans 8:14), churches are obliged to practice spiritual adoption through mentoring. Biblical mentoring is a way of passing on spiritual, financial, and emotional blessings as well as social capital to all families.

Congregations embarking on a journey of mentoring will discover they will receive many blessings as well. Biblically there is a clear vision of what mentoring looks like, especially where children are involved. In Luke 1:39–56, a mentoring relationship can be seen between Mary and Elizabeth's greetings and encounters when it comes to the birth of their children. In her joy, related to receiving the news of her being with child, Mary sought wisdom and affirmation from Elizabeth and was not disappointed, as the older woman gave what the teen mother needed. "The encounter between Mary and Elizabeth likewise underlines the place of key life transitions in the relationship between mentor and protégée. The two women's shared experience of pregnancy extends the bonds of kinship between them."[8] Going beyond a kinship bond to share mutual care and respect, as well as the care for children, can show churches how mentoring can reflect a type of "spiritual adoption" that is in the best interest of all involved.

## Church as Family

When children experience mutual love and respect between adult relationships in their lives, they too will benefit from these relationships. Terry W. York states, "A congregation cannot become the nurturing village it should be for its children until its identity and its responsibility in this regard are fully understood and embraced."[9] As York points out, it is the responsibility of the church, the ecclesiastical village, to nurture and pass on a spiritual legacy to young people. This means we, as believers, become spiritual siblings to each other. We are not just church and family, we become church as family! Passing on our faith is best done through intentional mentoring relationships that help form healthy identities in young people. For children that come from traumatic backgrounds, they must interact with many healthy adults to understand that healthy adults should be the

[8] Jean-Pierre Ruiz, "Luke 1:39–56: Mary's Visit to Elizabeth as Biblical Instance of Mentoring," *Apuntes* 17, no. 4 (January 1, 1997): 104.

[9] Terry W. York, "The Congregation as the Village," *Family And Community Ministries* 22, no. 4 (January 1, 2009): 10.

norm they never experienced! Adoptive parents—and in my case—a single adoptive parent cannot nurture and disciple children alone. Mentoring is critical to helping children navigate through trauma. When it comes to helping a protégée find her identity, the biblical example of Luke 1:43 models Elizabeth as helping Mary understand her identity as "the mother of the Lord."

## How the Church Can Be a Family to Adoptive and Foster Families

I was on church staff as a youth pastor at a medium sized church. Every year, our church held an event for married couples and their children. It was a sort of typical "marriage retreat" event—but for an evening. Married couples would come together, there would be worship, an encouraging message, dinner around the tables with other couples and even the children had their own program, so parents did not have to worry about getting a babysitter. As an exhausted, new single parent of a foster child moving toward adoption, I made the comment to my fellow pastors who ran the event, "The married couple night out is a great event and much needed. I sure could use a similar spiritually encouraging event as a single parent." Knowing how exhausted I was emotionally, physically, and spiritually while serving on staff, the response I received was, "We're just not ready to do anything like that yet." That's been about 12 years ago and, to my knowledge, that church has not done anything like the marriage night for single parents. Dr. Shelly Melia, in her chapter, has candidly pointed out the struggles of feeling like a second-class citizen in most churches.

Foster and adoptive families face unique, and often exhausting challenges. For foster families, their challenges can also be both emotionally and financially draining. As mentioned, foster children often come into the foster home having experienced significant trauma. Trauma can often play out through significant behavioral issues that can be consequential. These trauma-induced behaviors range from mild to severe, often creating consequences and family disruptions. Many foster and adoptive families face what is called the "honeymoon" period. My sons averaged approximately three months until the honeymoon period was over. Once the honeymoon period was over, my sons felt like they were in a safe place to "act upon their trauma." As a single parent, dealing with kids who exhibited misbehaviors due to trauma, I often felt very alone. I would get "the look" from parents whose children were well-behaved. It is easy to feel the weight of judgment—especially from church families who seem to "have it together."

There is a significant emotional toll foster parents face by having children come in and out of their home. I am grateful to these families who have been called to foster and not adopt. These are the homes where children can be placed because there is nowhere else for them to go. Foster (and adoptive) families are constantly having to navigate systems that are often dysfunctional and must advocate for children within the very systems that are supposed to help children. Rigid rules, red tape, and working with institutions that are not equipped to work with traumatized children often counter any potential progress foster and adoptive parents make in the life of children. Parents often face frustration in dealing with schools, child protective services, and other institutions that truly are not set up to help traumatized children. (The same can be said of churches.)

Further, if you have never fostered or adopted a child, you may not understand the difficult challenges of finding respite care for adopted children. You cannot just "get a babysitter." You had to have someone who was trained and approved to care for foster children. The typical process requires a potential babysitter or family members to go through the same 13-sessions of training adoptive and foster families undergo. Fortunately, many States have relaxed the requirements for finding a trusted sitter. Not to lose the point, it is still very much of a challenge for foster and adoptive parents to find babysitters or approved respite care. While there are certified respite care workers, they can be difficult to find geographically. A place that could serve to give foster and adoptive parents respite looks just like the marriage event I described above—except the focus could be on providing encouragement for foster, adoptive, or single parents.

Admittedly, I was jealous of the Married Couple night out. An evening of rest, encouragement, worship, fellowship, and a meal would have gone a long way to recharge me and my children! The ability to connect with other foster and adoptive parents is crucial in helping foster parents not give up. Maybe your church already has an investment in foster and adoptive ministries, maybe not. Either way, simply adding an encouraging event once or twice a year for foster and adoptive parents is something any church can do with a little bit of creativity.

Not everyone is called to foster or adopt children, but church members can play a significant part in nurturing the life of foster and adoptive parents and children. As a pastor, I am reminded of the importance of child dedication and baptism ceremonies in which parents, church leadership and church members all enter a covenant promise to nurture these children in the Christian faith. As a part of the beatitudes, when it comes to making an oath or entering a covenant, Jesus said, "All you need to say is simply 'Yes' or 'No'; anything beyond this comes from the evil one" (Matthew 5:37, NIV). In other words, if you do not stick to your word of nurturing all children who are brought into the life of God's family, you may very well be participating in evil.

## Simple Ways to Help

Here are some simplified ways to help:

1. Be mindful of your adoptive and foster families. If you notice parents seem exhausted, offer to take the kids to play or provide some sort of respite. It can be a challenge to do this as individuals but offering "Respite Nights" for foster and adoptive families can allow parents to get some rest.
2. Mentor a child. I cannot begin to tell you how important it is for adoptive and foster kids to have other adults to care about them outside of the family. Don't be afraid to build relationships with kids who need to see caring adults. Maybe you can be an "adoptive grandparent."
3. Offer to provide meals for the families. The daily grind can take its toll and even having someone cook a meal can make a huge difference. Simply having "one less task to do" can provide great encouragement to foster and adoptive families. Offering hospitality in this way shows families they are supported and not alone.
4. Don't make assumptions. We all have ideas of what caused children to come into the system, but it is important to set those assumptions aside and just get to know the children apart from the environments they came from. Also, as a single dad who has adopted, don't make assumptions about the parent(s). You may be surprised by their stories.
5. Understand the impact of trauma. Somewhere, I have heard it said, "The people that are the hardest to love need love the most." That is so true! Kids who come out of trauma need more patience and understanding. As I used to tell my leaders when it came to dealing with at-risk children and youth, "They are not the enemy, they are victims of the enemy." These kids, for a variety of reasons, have already felt the sting of rejection. The church should be the last place they feel that sting as well. See them as children who need extra nurturing to catch up on what they did not receive earlier in life.

6. Occasionally, host some gatherings for foster and adoptive parents. Offering times of fellowship and rest through a common meal can create much needed connections and support. Inviting a guest speaker to the meal who has navigated the roads of fostering and adoption can also be helpful. Some churches even host a Foster and Adoptive Parent support group.
7. These can all be summed up with this thought: if you are going to advocate for adoption, advocate for adoptive parents! Be a part of their team in some form or fashion. You don't have to KNOW what to do, but you can ask how you can help. It is worth mentioning once more what I put in a comment: "If you don't have empathy, I am okay with even receiving some sympathy because that sure beats apathy."

## Conclusion

Just as there are no perfect families, there are no perfect church families. However, even an imperfect church family can often be much healthier than the biological family a foster or adoptive child came from. As foster and adoptive parents, we are honestly just looking to be encouraged. We also want you, the rest of our church family, to understand that the children we love need time to overcome some of the harsh realities they face in their young lives. We need you to be patient. The fact is that even biological children can be extremely challenging to their biological parents. For those of us who have adopted children, we also want you to know that we love those children as if they were our own biological children. We love our children just like you love your children.

We don't expect our children to be perfect. We also know that sometimes the dynamics of our families can be different from most. We would rather have honest dialogue about our children and our families rather than the awkward, "We don't know what we can ask so we are just going to avoid you," type of behavior. If you want to begin to understand adoptive families, you can watch movies like, *Instant Family*. (I do have to warn you that there are some uncomfortable situations and bad language, but those things are mild compared to what our children have experienced.) We are willing to share what we can about our stories. Stories can often bring about understandings we did not previously have. We are willing to share with anyone who is willing to listen. Shelly's questions about single parents are just as applicable to foster and adoptive families: Do you see me? Do I belong here? Do you need me?

## References

Clark, Chap. *Adoptive Church: Creating an Environment Where Emerging Generations Belong*. Baker Academic, 2018.

Gianoulis, George C. "Is Sonship in Romans 8:14-17 a Link with Romans 9?" *Bibliotheca Sacra* 166, no. 661 (January 2009): 70–83.

Goodrich, John K. "'As Long as the Heir Is a Child': The Rhetoric of Inheritance in Galatians 4:1-2 and P. Ryl. 2.153." *Novum Testamentum* 55, no. 1 (2013): 61–76.

Miles, Jack. "Israel as Foundling: Abandonment, Adoption, and the Fatherhood of God." *Hebrew Studies*, 46 (2005): 7–24.

Peppard, Michael. "Adopted and Begotten Sons of God: Paul and John on Divine Sonship." *The Catholic Biblical Quarterly* 73, no. 1 (January 2011): 92.

Ruiz, Jean-Pierre. "Luke 1:39-56: Mary's Visit to Elizabeth as Biblical Instance of Mentoring." *Apuntes* 17, no. 4 (January 1, 1997): 104.

Shirley, Chris. *Family Ministry and the Church*. Randall House Publishing, 2018.

Wall, John. "Fallen Angels: A Contemporary Christian Ethical Ontology of Childhood." *International Journal of Practical Theology* 8, no. 2 (October 2004): 160–184.

York, Terry W. "The Congregation as the Village." *Family And Community Ministries* 22, no. 4 (January 1, 2009): 10.

## Chapter 5

# Engaging and Equipping Traditional Nuclear Families

Kevin Jones, Ed.D.

## New Family Ministry Paradigms

Consider this thought experiment with me for a moment. Imagine walking into a church building and scanning the rows, unable to distinguish which families are biologically related. You might think that ethnicity could make this task relatively straightforward, and if so, you're correct. However, this scenario is hypothetical; I'm not leaning toward a colorblind approach or diminishing the diverse ethnic identities and the unique ways in which the Lord created us. Scripture tells us that every nation, tribe, and tongue will bow at the feet of God. My question is: What if our families were so interconnected they weren't divided by seating arrangements or shared biology? Picture walking into a church where a nuclear family—husband, wife, and a few children—serves others within the local church community, such as widows, orphans, college students, and guests. They do so in such a manner that a widow doesn't appear as a widow, and a college student seamlessly fits into the family they spend time with. I believe this represents a new paradigm of church ministry.

## Family Ministry in the New Paradigm: It's Easier Than Being Stuck on an Iceberg

I've become fascinated with the ship, *Endurance*. This vessel is part of history, famously captained by E. S. Shackleton, who set out to accomplish something unimaginable. He aimed to take a ship and a crew to the most remote parts of the world. In 1915, this wasn't just dangerous—it was a venture into the unknown, and with the technology of that time, they were completely on their own. Twenty-eight men. A pack of dogs. A fully stocked ship. A family.

The book, now a documentary, about their journey, is filled with adventure, agony, and awe. Although this book does not fall into the Christian genre, some of the men clearly acknowledged God's power, with the Christians aboard reading the Bible to stay grounded. As the ship was sinking and each person was only allowed a few pounds of items, Shackleton took a few pages of his Bible for inspiration: Psalm 23 and a portion of Job.[1]

There were harrowing moments: men hunting seals and penguins for food, being hunted by leopard seals, hunted by their own hunger, dragging 20-footlong lifeboats across the Arctic. Walking across unforgiving and unending packs of frigid icebergs to stay alive. They needed one another. They needed God's grace. These are the kinds of things that make this story so compelling and applicable for church and family leadership and ministry.

There are a few lessons that stand out to me from this journey. First, the name of the ship—*Endurance*—is a powerful reminder. So many families today lack endurance—the ability to withstand difficulty and hardship. Families try to avoid the conditions that require endurance: adversity, hurt, pain, and prolonged stressful activity. Yet, the writer of Hebrews reminds us, "For you have need of endur-

[1] Alfred Lansing, *Endurance: Shackleton's Incredible Voyage* (McGraw Hill, 1959), 64–65.

ance, so that when you have done the will of God you may receive what is promised" (Hebrews 10:36, ESV).

Second, families need courageous, bold leaders—individuals who know how to build teams, leverage the strengths of each member, remain resilient in the midst of chaos, and draw others into their family to reflect God's vision of a church family. Some of Ernest Shackleton's leadership methods may have seemed unconventional, but they worked.

In a sense, unless one goes through a formal adoption process, we don't get to choose our families—or do we? In fact, we do. You can walk into your church this week and find people whose lives your family can speak into, and who can pour into yours in return. This is not to diminish the significance of formal adoption, but to remind us of what it means for the church to be a true family.

Many believers are abandoned or rejected by their biological families when they come to Christ, and the church becomes their only family. It is essential that we desire to build families, not based on flawed, worldly standards, but on the understanding that God calls us to journey through life together.

Remarkably, all the men on Shackleton's expedition survived for hundreds of days—on the sea, or rather, on the ice. Most of those days were marked by darkness and difficulty. Yet ultimately, they all survived. This reminds me of another reality I often observe in church families: many of our days may feel dark and difficult, but in the end, all who call on the name of our Lord and Savior, Jesus Christ, will be saved.

I'm not suggesting that every man on Shackleton's ship was a believer—just as we cannot assume Jonah's ship was filled only with believers. My point is this: all who call on the Lord's name and profess faith in Him will be saved. Though we may face challenges, turbulence, trials, and trauma, we are sustained by God's grace and His design for us to walk through life together—in family.

## Nuclear Family Research

Talcott Parsons argued that "the nuclear family is a social system,"[2] consisting of a heterosexual married couple and typically two to five children. He further suggested that this structure "can be distinguished and does function as a significant group."[3] While this traditional definition of the nuclear family may not align with how society views family structures today, it remains relevant in certain respects. Notably, Parsons emphasizes two key points: first, that adults are involved in the lives of children, and second, that the family unit is seen as a cohesive group. For Christians we take this a step further and say this family is made for the glory of God and should do acts of worship unto God.

Tony Evans states, "If we're ever to see the salvation of our nation, we must first pursue the salvation of the family. The strength or weakness of the family will ultimately determine whether our society stands or falls."[4] Some may argue that we (those in the United States) live in a post-Christian nation, while others might contend it is pre-Christian. Regardless, this book is not solely for those residing stateside; it is intended for a global audience, calling churches worldwide to action. For all families to think deeply about how they serve one another. Whether congregations gather in large buildings, under a tent, coffee shops, or schools, they are all tasked with the mission of proclaiming the name of Jesus Christ and fulfilling the Great Commission as family. With this objective in mind, we must prioritize the strengthening of families. This entails ensuring that no member of the local congregation feels isolated or lacks the sense of having a mother, father, brother, or sister. When the local church succeeds

---

[2] Talcott Parsons, *Family, Socialization and Interaction Process*, edited by Robert F. Bales (Free Press, 1956), 309.

[3] Parsons, *Family, Socialization and Interaction Process*, 308.

[4] Tony Evans and Jonathan Evans, *Kingdom Family Devotional: 52 Weeks of Growing Together* (Focus on the Family, 2016), VI.

in this mission, we can then work toward reinforcing the fabric and foundation of the communities in which we live and serve.

Nick Schulz, in *Home Economics: The Consequences of Changing Family Structure*, highlights the economic significance of the decline of the nuclear family. He noted: "in 1960, approximately 75% of adults over 18 were married, whereas by 2011, fewer than 50% of households consisted of married couples."[5] This has not changed much. According to usafacts.org:

> In 2024, 47.1% of households were headed by married couples, the second lowest share since 2022's all-time low of 46.8%. The percentage of households with a married couple peaked 75 years ago: in 1949, it was 78.8%. That percentage has been below 50.0% since 2010, when the rate was 49.7%. In other words, less than half of American households have included a married couple for over a decade.[6]

As we have spent time in this book, reimagining what church as a family looks like, I believe it's beneficial for intact biological families to understand that many individuals in your local church may share a similar family structure. These statistics are evidence of the change that needs to take place and should motivate us to connect with people outside of our own home or even church environment.

Schulz underscores that while dysfunction within the family may be a concern, it does not necessarily dictate an individual's future. Numerous factors (too many to name) influence an individual's future, and no single element guarantees success, just as a profound love for God does not safeguard one from issues. Many of you reading this book, like me, may come from families affected by divorce, and other

---

[5] Nick Schulz, *Home Economics: The Consequences of Changing Family Structure* (AEI Press, 2013), 21–26.

[6] "The State of Relationships, Marriages, and Living Alone in the US," *USAFacts*, last modified February 11, 2025, https://usafacts.org/articles/state-relationships-marriages-and-living-alone-us/.

forms of dysfunction, yet we remain, sustained by the Lord, filled with living water, and are used as conduits and tools through which rivers of living water flow because we are filled with the Holy Spirit. Furthermore, I refrain from measuring Christianity by the world's standards of success. My point is this: family is God's creation, and if it is God's idea, then I believe there are inherent advantages to it.[7] We understand, God is sovereign, and in His sovereignty can sustain all things without man's help. That does not take away from the fact that He gives us freedom and uses us as conduits of grace and giving.

The National Center for Family & Marriage Research shows similar statistics as above and goes deeper to show the groups most affected by this decline are Hispanic and Black women. The marriage rate for Hispanic women has decreased by 33%, while the rate for Black women has dropped by 60% during this time period.[8]Again, God can and has used fractured families, single men, and single women to do His will. He does not need a nuclear family to do His work, yet again, God created the family, which means it is important. Moreover, these statistics are not intended to evoke a sense of paternalism toward Hispanic and Black women specifically. It is to provoke a sense of godliness toward them. These groups have a long-standing tradition of faith, consistently placing their trust in the Lord and seeking His guidance.

**RG:** *I believe every single one of us who have contributed perspectives from "other family models" would agree that a family that has a mom and dad in an intact and loving relationship would be the ideal. We affirm this. In fact, I suspect we all wish*

[7] For those who regularly attend church, the divorce rate drops 25–50% below the national average, according to research by Shaunti Feldhahn and Tally Whitehead in *The Good News About Marriage: Debunking Discouraging Myths About Marriage and Divorce* (Multnomah, 2014).

[8] "Original Data," National Center for Family & Marriage Research, accessed November 12, 2024, https://www.bgsu.edu/ncfmr/resources/data/original-data.html.

*that we had the ideal … but we do not … and for many of us, it is emotionally painful. The last thing any of us want to feel is the weight of being "less than ideal" in the (church) family that should be loving us as fellow brothers and sisters in Christ. In fact, as Jesus was on the cross, He recognized that Mary would—for whatever reason—be in a less-than-ideal family…and He rectified this need by forming a family bond between Mary and John. "When Jesus saw his mother there, and the disciple whom he loved standing nearby, he said to her, "Woman, here is your son," and to the disciple, "Here is your mother." From that time on, this disciple took her into his home"* (John 19:26–27, NIV).

## Design

You think family is not important? Family is God's idea. "Household" or "family" in Scripture reflects a richness of meaning that reaches far beyond contemporary usage in public discourse. Without raising its importance to an idolatrous level yet affirming its foundational significance for the community, the Old Testament presents the family as a metaphor for God's relationship with Israel and as a vehicle of grace for human beings.[9] Again, imagine with me for a moment that each biological family, in some sense, makes a deliberate decision to invite others to become part of their family. It's important to note that this invitation is not based on any particular skill set, nor is it given with partiality, as James warns against such behavior. This act is simply about following what Jesus Christ instructed in Matthew. In Mark 10:29–31, Jesus declared, "Truly I say to you, there is no one who has left house or brothers or sisters or mother or father or children or lands, for my sake and for the gospel, who will not receive a hundredfold now in this time, houses and brothers and sisters and mothers and children and lands, with persecutions, and

[9] J. A. Dearman, "The Family in the Old Testament," *Interpretation* 52, no. 2 (1998): 117–129.

in the age to come eternal life. But many who are first will be last, and the last first" (ESV). Jesus Christ promised that we would gain a new family here, but He also cautioned that we would face persecutions and hardships along the way. The irony of this verse lies in Peter's seemingly selfish statement to Jesus about leaving everything behind to follow Him. However, instead of rebuking Peter harshly, Jesus gently reminded him of His promise: anyone who leaves their family for His sake will gain far more family within His kingdom. If you belong to a nuclear family, you should extend your familial bonds to include those who come to know Jesus Christ, especially those who have had to leave their biological families due to their newfound faith in Him. This passage emphasizes that Jesus considers His true family to be those who follow Him. In Matthew 12:48–50, Jesus redefined family by saying that those who do the will of His Father are His true mother, brothers, and sisters. This highlights the deep spiritual bond shared among believers, forming a family rooted in faith and obedience to God. The church, then, is not just a gathering place but a true spiritual family where relationships are shaped by commitment to God's will. While this doesn't mean we should neglect our biological families, Scripture clearly states that our true family consists of those united by the blood of Jesus Christ.

**JJ:** *It is important to understand the idea of "household" in the ancient world. In fact, there is no word in Hebrew, Greek, or Latin that likens the family to that of our nuclear family construct. Ancient households in the Old and New Testaments usually went beyond immediate family to include extended family, servants, and their families, and any foreigners or sojourners that might be dwelling with the household. While parent-child relationships were important, the bond between siblings in the ancient world was much deeper. This carries major implications for the church, in that it was these sibling relationships that Jesus and the ear-*

*ly church appropriate in their understanding of the church as a family and household of faith. It is within this idea of the "household of God" that early churches functioned as a surrogate family to one another. The group took precedence over the individual. It is likewise within this model that the church today can function in a healthy and holistic way. When the local church views itself as a surrogate family, much like ancient churches, it becomes a healthy and secure base for all generations, all individuals, and all kinds of families. An intentional, holistic, family ministry that involves all generations of the church can be a strong ally to help congregations function in this capacity.*

Imagine yourself sitting in your usual spot at church. We often don't change seats, although perhaps we should. As you sit there, you notice a new family entering, or perhaps a single person. As you scan the pew you also spot a widow or widower with whom you've never interacted much. Remember, the God of Heaven, who once walked this earth, promised us that we would gain brothers, sisters, mothers, and fathers, both in this life and in the life to come. So how well are we living out this promise of Christ? Do you truly embrace those who arrive without their biological families as your brothers, sisters, mothers, fathers, or children? We should, and we must.

Again, it's important to note that this invitation is not based on any particular skill set, nor is it given with partiality, as James warned against such behavior. James said, "My brothers and sisters, believers in our glorious Lord Jesus Christ must not show favoritism. Suppose a man comes into your meeting wearing a gold ring and fine clothes, and a poor man in filthy old clothes also comes in. If you show special attention to the man wearing fine clothes and say, 'Here's a good seat for you,' but say to the poor man, 'You stand there' or 'Sit on the floor by my feet,' have you not discriminated among yourselves and become judges with evil thoughts?" (James 2:1–4, NIV). James gave a stark warning and reminder because it is all too easy to want to spend time only with those who are easy to be around or with whom we share common interests. We often choose to be with people who don't come with baggage or who enjoy the same things we do, focusing solely on those who seem outwardly appealing. Let me remind you once again, brothers and sisters, that we are all sinful, depraved, and in desperate need of a Savior. One's outward appearance does not determine whether they are godly or ungodly.

Just as James warned us not to judge by appearances or gravitate only toward those who are comfortable and familiar, the call to reach the lost demands that we go beyond what is easy or conventional. The mission of the church is not limited to traditional models or safe environments but must reflect God's impartial love and bold pursuit of every soul. Shackleton's journey into the unknown mirrors the church's call to step into uncharted territory—where comfort is scarce, but God's presence is near. When we abandon favoritism and tradition-bound thinking, we open ourselves to be led by the Spirit into deeper, more transformative ministry.

E. S. and his crew would not have survived doing things the conventional way. Nor can our churches cling to every conventional and traditional model of church life and ministry and reach a new generation of unchurched, unconcerned, unregenerate image bearers. We must remember that, with God's hand upon us, we can accomplish marvelous things. He is our protector in the most difficult of circumstances. There was a pastor aboard the ship and as previously mentioned, E. S. himself had an acute awareness of God. His awareness and appreciation became more complete, not by remaining in the safety of land, but was revealed to him through trial and tumult of making camp on an iceberg. As God calls us into the unknown to reach the unconcerned, let us know that whatever we face, God the Holy Spirit is with us. He can keep us and kindle the hearts of those we engage. Moreover, He can and will present us to God the Father and Son with great joy.

## *Family Ministry* by Charles Sell

In the 1980s, Charles Sell, author of one of the first comprehensive family ministry texts, proposed a definition of family ministry emphasizing the role of education: "Family ministry involves communicating to people of all ages, in as many ways as possible, the biblical and practical truths of family living."[10] The focus here was on communication to all people. Not just people found under one's own roof. The focus was inward, outward, upward, and forward. The focus was biblical and practical; orthodoxy, orthography, and ontological.

## *Family Ministry: A Comprehensive Guide* by Diana Garland

In the 1990s, Diana Garland constructed a sociological framework for family ministry. She explained:

> This book is designed to provide church leaders with a foundation for designing and carrying out congregational ministries with and through families. Its basic premise is that *ministry leadership is most effective when it calls out and builds on the strength of families and congregations.* Family ministry needs to be grounded in an understanding of family life in today's social and cultural context.[11]

Diana Garland asserts, with research-backed evidence, that North American families are experiencing a crisis. Drawing on her experience serving in local churches and teaching at the university level, Garland argues that Christian families are strengthened when they are rooted and nurtured within their congregations. The first

[10] Charles M. Sell, *Family Ministry* (Zondervan, 1980), 64.

[11] Diana R. Garland, *Family Ministry: A Comprehensive Guide* (InterVarsity Press, 1999), 11 (emphasis in the original).

edition of her book was published in 1999, and I recall experiencing significant personal growth from reading it as a student. The second edition was released in 2012, featuring updated research and organizing her insights into four main categories: the context of family ministry, family formation, family dynamics, and leading family ministry. The scholarly work in this book is exceptional, as Garland explores the historical, sociological, theological, and biblical aspects of Christianity and family ministry within the local church. If you are looking for the *why* of how things are taking place within families in the United States and trends in family ministry, this is a great tool.

### *Practical Family Ministry: A Collection of Ideas for Your Church* by Timothy Paul Jones and John David Trentham

Timothy Paul Jones, along with other contributors, provides numerous practical approaches for families to engage in ministry both within and beyond their homes.[12] The primary aim of the book is to equip church leaders so they can, in turn, enable family members to undertake the work of discipling at home. These authors have served in diverse church settings and recognize that cultivating a church family does not occur naturally or effortlessly. Therefore, they offer practical strategies for churches to fulfill God's calling. Readers are reminded of God's design for family and discipleship.

### *Perspectives on Family Ministry: Three Views* by Timothy Paul Jones, et al.

*Perspectives on Family Ministry,*[13] now in its second edition, examines various methods churches employ to engage families both within and beyond their congregations. The authors argue for what they believe is the most biblically accurate approach, advocating for a specific perspective on family ministry. This engaging book serves

[12] Timothy Paul Jones and John David Trentham, eds., *Practical Family Ministry: A Collection of Ideas for Your Church* (Randall House Publication, 2015).

[13] Timothy Paul Jones, et al., *Perspectives on Family Ministry*, 2nd ed. (B&H Academic, 2022).

as a valuable tool or resource for individuals reflecting on, developing, modifying, or transitioning from one form of family ministry to another.

### *Family Ministry and the Church: A Leader's Guide for Ministry Through Families* by Chris Shirley

Chris Shirley serves as a pastor, preacher, and professor, significantly contributing to scholarship, practical theology, and our popular area's mainstream discussions on family ministry. Shirley's book is an excellent resource for ministry leaders as well as college and seminary students.[14] It covers topics such as his working definition of family ministry and strategies for equipping pastors and other leaders within the congregation to strengthen marriages, support parents and grandparents, and address contemporary family issues. What I appreciate most about this work is its deep theological and practical framework for ministry leaders. His work illustrates what a healthy church and ministry should look like for families.

### *Family Discipleship: Leading Your Home Through Time, Moments, and Milestones* by Matt Chandler and Adam Griffin

This book delivers precisely what its title promises.[15] Many families find themselves in need of guidance, especially as they experience challenging periods, joyous occasions, and various milestones that depend on their children's ages or their family dynamics. Chandler and Griffin encourage us to cultivate sustainable rhythms of gospel-centered discipleship. Concentrating on the three key areas highlighted in the subtitle, the book provides numerous suggestions to assist both young and mature families in contemplating the development of family discipleship. It challenges parents and pastors

[14] Chris Shirley, *Family Ministry and the Church: A Leader's Guide for Ministry Through Families* (Randall House Publication, 2018).

[15] Matt Chandler and Adam Griffin, *Family Discipleship: Leading Your Home Through Time, Moments, and Milestone* (Crossway Publishing, 2020).

to create strategic, unique, and comprehensive plans tailored to each family within the church community.

### *Family Discipleship That Works: Guiding Your Child to Know, Love, and Act Like Jesus* by Brian Dembowczyk

In *Family Discipleship That Works*, Brian Dembowczyk shares some eye-opening statistics.[16] For example, 64% of teens don't believe the Bible is accurate in all it teaches. This data offers a clear snapshot of what we're up against in discipling the next generation. For instance, many teens question the sinlessness of Jesus, and trust in the church. Some 42% don't believe God is an all-powerful, all-knowing Creator. Additionally, 79% of teens believe good people can earn their way into Heaven, a misconception we must work hard to address. Sadly, most young adults have stopped attending church altogether, but many are now seeking. Another staggering statistic is 43% of young adults don't consider faith important, and fewer than 1 in 10 list faith as their top priority. This is the context in which we are discipling today. Brian offers some evidenced-based research and paths forward to address the current climate of teens and young adults.

## Book Summary Conclusion

Each of these books are really helpful tools that point toward how families can serve and flourish. Each book is also packed with insightful information. I encourage complete reading of them all. However, each one would wholeheartedly (or should) agree with Cope who states, "A family is humanity's great opportunity to walk the way of the cross."[17] The way of the cross means we take up our own crosses daily. It means from birth to death we live lives sacrificially. It means

[16] Brian Dembowczyk, *Family Discipleship That Works: Guiding Your Child to Know, Love, and Act Like Jesus* (IVP, 2024).

[17] Henry Frederick Cope, *Religious Education in the Family* (Abingdon Press, 1915), 4.

families are willing to sacrifice what may be compatible for what is best for others. It means families walk in self-denial, humility, and collective gentleness. The Cross is not just a point in history. The cross is a way of life. It also means we help bear the burdens of others. Families often focus on flourishing, improving one another, sending children to college, building businesses, or being successful in their respective fields. However, we frequently overlook the fact that family provides a unique opportunity to share in each other's burdens. To truly support others, we must become intimately involved in their lives. Bearing someone's burden requires being present with them when they need help carrying a heavy load.

Recently, as I was moving furniture into the house by myself, my family arrived. My son stepped in to help carry the furniture, sharing the burden with me. This practical scenario illustrates the importance of proximity and strength. Despite not wanting to do it, my son helped anyway. While bearing burdens is not easy, and sometimes you may not feel like it, it is vital for us to be present for one another, even when we don't feel like it. As Christ instructed, by doing so, we fulfill the law.

Cope goes on to say, "Methods of securing family efficiency will not be discovered by accident. If it is worthwhile to study the minor details, such as baking cakes and sweeping floors, surely it is even more important to study the larger problems of organization and discipline."[18] There is a science of home-direction and an art of family living; both must be learned with patient study. I urge you to expand your thinking beyond just your immediate biological family when considering how to enhance family efficiency. Our churches often struggle with inefficiency because we fail to implement the principles found in 1 Peter 4. This chapter instructs us that, above all, we should love one another earnestly, for love covers a multitude of sins (1 Peter 4:8). We are called to offer hospitality without complaint and to

[18] Cope, *Religious Education in the Family*, 6.

use our diverse gifts to serve one another, acting as faithful stewards of God's grace. If we, as members of our local churches, commit to loving one another, forgiving each other's sins, being hospitable without grumbling, and using our gifts, we can achieve the goal of an efficient church family. Are you utilizing your skills and gifts to glorify God and serve within your local church community? If so, continue this commendable work. If not, find a way to start using your gifts to serve others in your church community immediately.

## Family Ministry

The Bible affirms the centrality of the family unit doing the work of passing the faith from one generation to the next. Family ministry is the work of the Gospel in and through a family. Nonetheless, as a culture we may have excluded others around us trying to honor the words in Deuteronomy 6:5–7 and Psalm 78. Here's a quick question for reflection: *What families are you doing life with?* Our families were never meant to live in isolation. The gospel calls us to live in community with others, modeling loyalty, faithfulness, and trust in both big and small ways. As we make these practices a part of our daily lives, we help our kids understand what true, committed relationships look like—both with God and with others.

I've served as a pastor, and I've been involved in churches long enough to know that organizationally, it can be challenging to figure out how to move the whole church in a new direction. But I want to offer a simple suggestion: Just start. Today. I'm not saying you should go back to your church and immediately try to overhaul and start a new ministry changing the entire paradigm of the church. Unless of course, that is what is needed. That's not what I'm talking about. What I'm asking is this: What family do you do life with? What families are you in community with, supporting one another in faith?

**RG:** *This is an excellent question and one that needs further explanation. As this book has tried to share, and as Kevin has so poignantly pointed out to us—family goes beyond biology. We must begin to define family not only biologically, but theologically. When we do this, we can go beyond the church-imposed boundaries of various segregated groups. As Paul stated in Colossians 3:11, we are all one in Christ's family! This teaching breaks down our rigid definitions of who we accept as family—beyond biology, ethnicity, culture, denominations, and age-segregation!*

The key here is being obedient to the Lord and modeling for our children that we are not meant to be self-reliant. Our strength doesn't come from within ourselves; it comes from the Lord and from our spiritual brothers and sisters. This is something we need to show through our actions.

Take Paul's words in Romans 1:11: "I long to see you, that I may … strengthen you" (ESV). Who is strengthening your faith on a daily or weekly basis? We need each other. We get our strength from God and from the community of believers we walk alongside. This is where we learn to trust and rely on God more fully.

Let's also look at Proverbs 3:6: "In all your ways acknowledge Him, and He will make straight your paths" (ESV). Acknowledging God in all things is essential. It's our responsibility to teach our children the power of a gospel-centered family—where every decision, every conversation, and every action is done in a way that acknowledges God. This is how we show them what it looks like to live a life fully reliant on God. In the end, it's not about a big program or a sweeping change. It's about the families we do life with and how we model, day in and day out, the reality that our strength and guidance come from God and from the community of believers who walk with us.

## Family and Ministry in the New Paradigm

The paradigm of family ministry has shifted significantly over the past two decades. The changes in culture, technology, marriage rates, and family structure require a new approach to ministry. Families today are busier than ever, with extracurricular activities and technology consuming much of their time. This shift has impacted how we approach family ministry and discipleship. Whereas families once had more dedicated time for devotional activities, today, the challenge is to integrate faith into the rhythms of daily life.

One significant change is the shift in how families engage with education and both secular and sacred information. In the past, teachers and parents were the primary source of information, but now students, teens, and children have access to virtually any information they need with a quick online search. As a result, the role of parents and church leaders has shifted from being information providers to guides who help young people interpret and apply knowledge within a biblical framework. I'm not suggesting that families can forego their responsibility in educating their children. Rather, I'm emphasizing that a four-year-old today, who is adept at using a cell phone or iPad, can access a wealth of information that would have been unreachable for a four-year-old two decades ago.

Technology has also drastically changed the way families interact. For some families, there is no interaction. Whereas families once gathered around the television for limited programming (30–60 minutes), today's digital world offers constant distractions. Are you old enough to remember when TV programming used to go off? It was a time when there was not constant digital streaming.? The constant distractions make it exceptionally challenging for families to engage in any form of interaction. There is a lack of discussion on matters of faith, and no opportunity to debrief each student's day to address social, emotional, or spiritual issues. Families miss the chance to reflect on how to love and nurture others within their community and church because we fail to make time for meaningful interaction. Regarding technology, I strongly encourage implementing no-tech hours, days, and designated areas within your home to facilitate deep conversations. If this concept is new to you and you're considering establishing no-tech times, I advise replacing them with thoughtful questions, devotional time, or resources to inspire family discussions. Numerous resources are readily available, easily found with a quick search.

Additionally, the rise of year-round extracurricular activities has further encroached on family time. We need to reimagine how family can flourish in the midst of extracurricular activities. First, the LORD said, "Remember the Sabbath day, to keep it holy"(Exodus 20:8, ESV). The term *holy* refers to something that is set apart, sacred, or distinct from the everyday routines and practices of our lives. Unfortunately, for most Christian families, the Sabbath holds no special significance and has become much like any other day of the week. In my view, the traditional approach to family ministry or activities often involves loading up little Johnny and traveling to a nearby city for an all-day baseball or soccer event on Sundays. I believe the new model of family ministry should involve reclaiming the Sabbath, keeping it holy, and choosing to miss little Johnny's baseball tournament on a Sunday in order to dedicate Sundays to serving the Lord. I did not say, "remember the Sabbath and keep it holy," God did.

While this can be seen as a negative, and I think it has and can have profound negative impacts on families, extra curricula can also provide new opportunities for ministry. Families can now engage in gospel-centered conversations and discipleship during these activities, using the time to be intentional about their faith and witness. So, if you have to be at an event, Monday to Saturday, make time to talk about the Lord with the people around you.

**RG:** *For the reasons Kevin listed, and more, American culture is increasingly secular, and many families have stopped "going to church" regularly. This is another reason we are advocating for "Reimagining Church as Family." As church membership and attendance decline, so do church participation and church budgets. Staffing will look different. If a church has a moderate to large size congregation, they may be able to afford multiple staff. However, smaller churches will require staffing that is bi- or co-vocational. In other words, staffing may look more like a one-position family ministry pastor rather than separate youth, children, and family pastors. Co-vocational may also look like a youth pastor who also leads worship services. Other churches will need to heavily lean on volunteers. These realities affirm that volunteers will need to have some deeper theological training and understanding. Growing leaders requires that we all engage in discipleship and Christian nurture. Further giving young people ownership of their own faith by allowing them to participate and be involved, rather than just spectate, increases the probability of continued spiritual leadership. When churches make comments like, "Youth are the future of the church," but do nothing to prepare youth to lead, it is a very empty sentiment.*

You have the power to engage with someone tomorrow, to disciple a young person in your community, or to choose how you spend your time. I often hear people say they don't have time, for one thing or another, as related to serving Christ, but we always have the capacity to say yes or no to the commitments we make. Priority is priority.

## Prioritizing—Tips for Nuclear Families

1. *"Read" the Word Daily With Your Family.* The first step is simple but powerful: read the Bible together every day. When

I first got married, I thought I needed to prepare a sermonette every morning. I quickly realized that wasn't realistic. What I needed to do and still do is read the Bible daily with my wife and now family. Today, I focused on just opening the Word and reading it with my kids. There are many devotionals out there, but the core idea is to make Scripture a daily part of your family's routine. Once again, this book is not intended to point us to those solely living under my roof—nor is my Bible reading. I engage with the Bible alongside individuals who do not reside in my home by using a Bible app, specifically with the young men I disciple. We follow the same Bible reading plan and frequently discuss the daily readings through text messages, group chats, and especially during times when they join us for dinner at my house.

2. *Plan Family Devotions—Even If It's Just Ten Minutes.* One of the most common struggles parents face is finding time for family devotions. With kids ranging from toddlers to teenagers, busy schedules can make it feel impossible. But here's my advice: get everyone up 15–20 minutes earlier. It's not glamorous, and no one really wants to do it, but that small adjustment can make a huge difference. It's often the simplest solutions that are the hardest to implement, but when we make the Bible a priority, we find a way.

I know this can be a challenge. My children's schedules are different—my older two need to be at school by 7:15 a.m., while my youngest starts at 9:00 a.m. But my youngest is required to be up by 6:00 or 6:15 a.m. so we can have a few quiet moments to prepare our hearts before the day begins. If we can make time for so many other things—sports, school, and work—why can't we prioritize spending time in the Word?

My wife is an exceptional host, and we thoroughly enjoy welcoming guests into our home. Whether you visit us for a short stay or an extended period, we're going to engage in discussions about Scripture. We view the college students, singles, and even other married couples from our church as part of our family. After Sunday service, our home often fills with numerous guests, and we usually converse about Scripture over a meal—during and after. As you reflect on your family devotions, consider including those who don't live under your roof. A question as simple as, "What is the Lord teaching you through His Word?" spurs on great conversation. And by the way, no phones or electronic devices at the table.

3. *Reset Your Priorities for Family Ministry. We need to take a step back and re-evaluate how we're doing family ministry. How are we planning time to be together? It's easy to get caught up in the rush of life, but our children need us to set the pace and prioritize what matters most. This means that even when schedules are hectic, we need to make a concerted effort to slow down and spend time in the Word together as a family. Our kids are watching, and when they see us make time for the Bible, they'll learn to value it too.*

**JJ:** *Just as Kevin addresses the need to re-evaluate and reset priorities as families, we must also do the same in family ministry as a church. Many times, our ministries in our churches add to the busyness and competition for parents and their time. Our kids ministry and student ministries do not talk to each other, neither do our family ministries and adult ministries. What if we all worked together and shared planned programs, classes, events, and especially resources for parents? Instead of planning multiple things requiring their attention and attendance—many of them similar in purpose—what if the ministries of the church worked* ***together*** *to honor families' precious time? At our church, our groups ministry and family ministry realized we had been* *trying to reach the same people—parents. We have now begun to work together to not compete for their time and to plan in concert and collaboration. This is the heart and idea of "interdependent family ministry" where ALL ministries of the church work together to own both family ministry and the church as a family.*

4. *Provide Resources for Daily Bible Study for Your Kids.* Lastly, it's important to equip our children with tools to study the Bible on their own. As they grow, we want them not to only hear Scripture but engage with it personally. There are great resources available—devotionals, Bible apps, and study tools—for children of all ages. Putting these in their hands shows them that spending time in the Word is not just a family activity, but a lifelong habit.
5. *It's Not Just Our Job—It's Our Role to Teach What Is Good.* But beyond that, I believe it's important for us to provide resources for our kids.

   What I mean by that is: My kids expect that we're going to talk about the things of God. It's a part of our rhythm. Talking about God's Word should feel natural, not forced. The sooner you start making these conversations a part of daily life, the better. It becomes something they just know is part of their routine—because they hear about it regularly at home.

   Let me also say, kids are exposed to ungodly things earlier than we often realize. In public schools or other public spaces, they hear about drugs, sex, and all sorts of negative influences at younger ages than we want them to. Sometimes it's through whispers on the playground or from friends using profanity they've picked up. You might hear your child come home and use a word they've never heard from you. You'll ask, "Where did you get that from?" and they'll tell you, "Johnny said it."

It's important to be proactive—prepare them for these things before they're exposed to them.

So, give your kids the resources and the conversations that will strengthen their faith. Set them on the path to know and love God's Word, because that's the foundation that will protect them in a world full of distractions.

## Being a Family for Those Who Have None

In this new paradigm of family ministry, it's essential that families engage with those who may not have a traditional family structure. This includes single individuals, widows, orphans, young adults, adoptive and foster families, and others who may lack close familial connections. We are called to bring them into our families, sharing life with them and offering support, just as we would for our own biological family members. The church must embrace its role as a spiritual family, offering belonging, care, and discipleship to all who need it.

This approach requires intentionality. It means inviting a young person into your home for dinner, mentoring a single adult, or offering support to a widow. It means prioritizing relationships that extend beyond biological connections, demonstrating the love of Christ in tangible ways.

## Building Trust in Family Ministry

One of the challenges in family ministry today is rebuilding trust. There is a growing distrust in institutions, including the church, due to scandals and unhealthy practices in some communities. In the past, families would often drop their children off at church programs without much thought. However, the paradigm has shifted. Today, trust must be built through genuine relationships and transparency. Families need to see the church as a place where they can be vulnerable, supported, and mentored in their faith.

As church leaders and families, we must recognize that the nuclear family is no longer the norm in many communities. Instead, family ministry must be comprehensive and adaptable, welcoming all types of family structures. In a world where family dynamics are increasingly complex, the church must be a place where all people can experience the love of Christ and find support, whether they have traditional family structures or not.

## Conclusion

In the context of modern church ministry, the nuclear family plays a critical role in shaping the spiritual direction and vibrancy of both individual lives and the church as a whole. In a time when the church is facing new challenges and shifts in paradigms, gospel-centered families can provide a powerful means to revitalize and support the church's mission. As we conclude this chapter, I will explore the role of the nuclear family in fostering spiritual growth within the home and how they can serve the church by prioritizing Bible engagement, family ministry, and Christ-like relationships. Additionally, we will consider strategies for families to model faith and discipleship, helping to meet the unique needs of today's church community.

### The Role of the Nuclear Family in Serving the Church

The nuclear family has a vital role in serving the church by being a model of gospel-centered living. Families who prioritize Bible reading, prayer, and spiritual discussions set an example for others, showing how to make faith central to family life. By sharing the struggles, joys, and victories of walking with Christ, families can help one another grow in faith.

Moreover, families who model Christlike behavior can serve the church by providing a witness of how the gospel transforms daily life. Through acts of service, hospitality, and community engagement, families show the church what it looks like to live out the Great Commission in the context of their homes and neighborhoods.

## Preparing the Next Generation for Ministry

In the new paradigm of church ministry, it's essential to focus on preparing the next generation to live out their faith and engage in ministry. This involves more than simply teaching them theological truths but equipping them to serve the church and their communities. Parents should be intentional in involving their children in ministry activities and conversations about how they can serve others. This might include participating in local service projects, hosting Bible studies, or helping with church events. By involving children in ministry from a young age, families help to cultivate a heart for service and a lifelong commitment to the church. The nuclear family, when committed to gospel-centered living, can serve as the first line of discipleship and ministry preparation, equipping children to become active participants in the life of the church.

As we look toward the future of family ministry, it is clear that the paradigm has shifted. The family is no longer just a biological unit; it is a broader community that includes the church and others who may not have traditional family structures. The power of a gospel-centered family lies in its ability to influence and transform lives, and it is through this lens that families can engage in ministry. By building trust, prioritizing relationships, and welcoming others into our lives, families can continue to be a force for good in the kingdom of God.

> **LF:** Even in the biological unit, the definition needs to be broader than simply parents and children. The church needs to recognize the great benefit of engaging grandparents, even aunts and uncles, in the responsibility of passing on faith to future generations.

As we embrace this new paradigm of family ministry, let us remember the words of Jesus in Mark 10:29–30: "there is no one who has left house or brothers or sisters or mother or father or children or lands, for my sake and for the gospel, who will not receive a hundredfold now in this time, … and in the age to come eternal life" (ESV). Families, both biological and spiritual, have the power to engage in the new paradigm of ministry, bringing the love of Christ to a world in need.

Additionally, nuclear families could also extend their influence by partaking in structured inter-family discipleship, whereby more seasoned families guide and reinforce the spiritual maturity of newer or struggling ones. This mentorship can range from family Bible studies to prayer partnerships, fostering spiritual accountability and resilience within the church community. In this vein, nuclear families concern the intentional investment of time. Presence is a potent gift; thus, families should strive to intentionally include others in their routines, inviting them for dinners, on family outings, or even during mundane daily activities such as grocery shopping. Such inclusivity conveys a robust message of love and acceptance, reducing isolation and creating a network of allies in faith and life.

Nuclear families have the opportunity to set an example in conflict resolution and forgiveness. By embodying these principles within their homes and involving others in discussions around managing disagreements in a God-honoring way, they contribute to a culture of peace and understanding grounded in the biblical admonition to live at peace with all men. Nuclear families could be to actively participate in intercessory prayer for other families and individuals in their church and broader community. Organizing prayer circles or chains reinforces the collective power of prayer, bringing comfort to those in need and strengthening the faith of the community as a whole.

Practicing open-hearted hospitality acts as a pivotal axis for the nurturing of deep relationships. Families can practice inviting others into their homes, not merely when everything is in perfect order, but in the authentic messiness of life. This openness breaks down barriers and fortifies bonds, urging acceptance and intimacy reflective of Christ's unyielding grace.

Lastly, nuclear families are encouraged to involve themselves in ongoing advocacy for inclusivity within the church's practices and events. This means championing programs and experiences that acknowledge and celebrate the spectrum of family structures and individual experiences within the church, thus ensuring a cohesive and comprehensive community spirit.

In summation, the new paradigm of family ministry invites nuclear families to become integral catalysts for communal growth, fostering connections that reflect the heart of Christ's teachings. Through active support, shared resources, comprehensive practices, and continuous spiritual engagement, these families can help construct a church environment where every member, irrespective of their familial circumstance, feels valued, supported, and loved.

**References**

Chandler, Matt, and Adam Griffin. *Family Discipleship: Leading Your Home Through Time, Moments, and Milestones*. Crossway Publishing, 2020.

Cope, Henry Frederick. *Religious Education in the Family*. Abingdon Press, 1915.

Dearman, J. A. "The Family in the Old Testament." *Interpretation* 52, no. 2 (1998): 117–129.

Dembowczyk, Brian. *Family Discipleship That Works. Guiding Your Child to Know, Love, and Act Like Jesus*. IVP, 2024.

Evans, Tony, and Jonathan Evans. *Kingdom Family Devotional: 52 Weeks of Growing Together.* Focus on the Family, 2016.

Feldhahn, Shaunti, and Tally Whitehead. *The Good News About Marriage: Debunking Discouraging Myths About Marriage and Divorce.* Multnomah: 2014.

Garland, Diana R. *Family Ministry: A Comprehensive Guide.* InterVarsity Press, 1999.

Jones, Timothy Paul, and John David Trentham. *Practical Family Ministry: A Collection of Ideas for Your Church.* Randall House Publication, 2015

Jones, Timothy Paul, et al. *Perspectives on Family Ministry.* 2nd ed. B&H Academic, 2022.

Lansing, Alfred. *Endurance: Shackleton's Incredible Voyage.* McGraw-Hill, 1959.

National Center for Family & Marriage Research. "Original Data." Accessed November 12, 2024. https://www.bgsu.edu/ncfmr/resources/data/original-data.html.

Parsons, Talcott. Family, *Socialization and Interaction Process.* Edited by Robert F. Bales. Free Press, 1956.

Schulz, Nick. *Home Economics: The Consequences of Changing Family Structure.* AEI Press, 2013

Sell, Charles M. *Family Ministry.* Zondervan, 1980.

Shirley, Chris. *Family Ministry and the Church: A Leader's Guide for Ministry Through Families.* Randall House Publication, 2018.

*USAFacts.* "The State of Relationships, Marriages, and Living Alone in the US." Last modified February 11, 2025, https://usafacts.org/articles/state-relationships-marriages-and-living-alone-us/.

# Parting Thoughts and Conclusion

## A Word About Knitting for Jesus

Having spent years in youth ministry and learning from many mistakes, I (Rich) realize the necessity of being flexible. This becomes more true the older I get. This reality, and this book, reminds me of a story from my younger years of ministry. I would often tell my leaders that our mission focus was clear. I would not spend my time "knitting for Jesus." This meant that if someone were to come up to me and say, "Pastor, we need a knitting for Jesus class for the youth." Unless this were a small group ministry where kids were enthralled with knitting and meet the purposes of evangelism and discipleship, my response would be, "I do not know about knitting so, please do not expect me to run around and purchase knitting supplies." After becoming a college professor and taking a part-time, lead pastor position for the first time, I realized there were actually "knitting for Jesus" ministries.

As I came into my new church and, of course, one of the first individuals to approach me said, "Pastor, we have a ministry where we knit various items like tissue box covers and footies for some of our shut-ins at the local nursing homes." This well-intentioned saint of a woman proceeded to show me the entire room of knitting materials which, in her defense, was a huge ministry at some point. Then, as the case often is, many in the "knitting circle" left. Not to be too morbid, but some had passed away or had become shut-ins themselves. She went on to explain, "For the past several years, we have been trying to get people to join us. The preachers have made announcements from the front (we all know how successful that approach is), but no one comes forward and now, nobody will even take our items." I did not mean for the following comment to come across as harsh as it did, but my ill-conceived response was, "Then why are you all (only two people) still doing this?" I had instant regret as I realized I had hurt her feelings. I apologized and stated that offense was not my intent.

Over the course of several weeks as I tried to repair the relationship, I was able to meet with the saintly woman again. The church, as many aging and declining churches do, stated that they wanted to attract younger families. Now, I am an "idea" person. I am horrible at details, but I love brainstorming and implementing new ideas. The county where we lived had the worst foster-care record in the state. There were less than 20 foster families and over 300 children in foster care for that county alone! Our church was located not too far from the big hospital. As I re-engaged with the lady, I stated, "As you know, our church really wants to bring in some younger families and, as you know, families in this county could use some kindness. Why don't we re-develop the knitting team to knit booties, caps, and scratch mittens for families who have babies born in our local hospital? We can even attach a card that says, "Our church LOVES families" and put the name, address, and contact information on the card. Suspiciously, the congregation member said, "Let me talk to my partner and see what she says."

It should be noted; I had never met her knitting partner since I had been at the church. A week and a half later, I received a face-to-face response from the congregation member. The basic message was, "We are NOT going to knit these items and give them to unwed mothers!" I was shocked and a bit flabbergasted. First, I never said anything about "unwed mothers" (though I would have been happy to give those items *especially* to unwed mothers). My second thought was, "Isn't this a better use of your skills and potentially connecting younger families to the church? After all, older folks walking around in knitted footies on waxed floors at a nursing home doesn't sound very safe to me!" (Yes, I have a cynical side.) My final thought (also cynical) was, "The attitude of not being willing to serve 'the least of these' was clearly the root of the aging church dying."

In some ways, we are in a different day and age. The advent of social media and many aspects of the digital revolution have changed our societies. However, in many ways, human beings still need to belong. We still need to be loved. We still need to be forgiven. We still need redemption and most importantly, we still need Jesus. Societies and cultures have always been "less than the ideal." Even the "heroes and heroines" of the Bible and our faith were all "less than ideal" (except Jesus). Yet God chose to use every single one of them. God used a prostitute named Rahab to continue the lineage of David and ultimately, Jesus. Speaking of David, he broke just about every one of the ten commandments through his actions and after actions with Bathsheba—and yet David is declared "...a man after God's own heart" (1 Samuel 13:14; Acts 13:22). The church is still called to care for orphans and widows (James 1:27; Acts 6:1–6), the foreigner among us (Deuteronomy 16:14; 26:11; Leviticus 25:35) and those among us who are different (Hebrews 13:1–2) for we never know when we are "entertaining angels." In other words, we are biblically called to minister to families of all constructs—not just post-World War II nuclear families.

Maybe in an effort to be relevant, we have undertaken approaches that have been culturally relevant (not a bad thing) but have forgotten how to be biblically relevant and obedient (that is a bad thing). Recalling the history of the development of youth and children's ministry, there was a need to re-examine how the church and society were neglecting the needs of the most vulnerable. Para-church ministries sprang up and created vibrant and much needed ministry to youth and children. As churches eventually took note of parachurch "successes," expert practitioners professionalized ministry to meet age and stage-specific needs. Now, perhaps we have "thrown the baby out with the bath." (A nod to all my former students.) Maybe it is time to recover the theological definition of what it means to be "the family of God" and recognize, as Dr. Chap Clark points out, we are all spiritual siblings—no matter what our earthly family constructs looks like.

We have laid out biblical reasons not to only be "church and family," but to also become "church *as* family." As we become older and "wiser," maybe we can see appropriate seasons when we engage in "knitting for Jesus"—for the right reasons. We do not need more "programs," but we do need to recognize that our world is far from ideal. Many people are living in circumstances that are less than ideal, but real. Some of those reasons are God-ordained. Maybe some of those reasons are not, but if God is calling a "Rahab" to do His work and become a part of the lineage of Jesus, who are we not to think outside of our little boxes? After all is said and done, the "qualification" of entering Heaven is not a socially constructed model of family, it is whether we are in the family of God through Jesus Christ.

## A Big, Messy, Eternal Family

The NBC series *Parenthood* chronicled the lives and account of the Braverman family. The legacy of Zeek Braverman and Camille Braverman, the show's respective patriarch and matriarch, is manifest in their four grown children and their families. Due to the show's often authentic portrayal of the ups and downs, victories, and struggles of the Braverman clan, it struck a chord of commonality among America's viewing public. In an episode from the show's fourth season, Julia Braverman-Graham and her husband finally get the news that the adoption of Victor, a boy they have had in foster care, is going to finally happen. In a very private event that traditionally includes only the adoptee and his adopters, the entire Braverman clan noisily interrupts in order to make their presence known and to be a part of the ceremony. In this emotional scene, Victor's new family tells him of the benefits of becoming a Braverman. His grandfather promises to teach him to field the hot grounder, his aunt promises to teach him about girls, while his cousin promises to undo all that the aunt teaches. One by one, countless other family members take turns encouraging him as the newest member of the family. Victor finally belongs, and nothing solidifies this more than when he calls Julia "Mom" as he runs from the chamber with his new sister and cousins to the vending machines. As Zeek is walking out, the judge tells him, "That's a beautiful family you've got there." He proudly, yet simply, replies, "They're something, aren't they?"[1]

What a beautiful picture of the big, messy, interdependent family called the church! Whether Hollywood was intentional or not, this final scene in the judge's chamber is a glorious picture of our adoption in Christ and into the family of God. Family ministry is for every one of us, because we are indeed an eternal family; and it will take every ministry in the local church working together in interdependence to eventually reframe the narrative and tell a new story of the church as a family.

[1] *Parenthood.* "Because You're My Sister," Season 4, episode 15. Originally aired January 22, 2013.

## Author Biographies

**Larry Fowler** is the founder of the Legacy Coalition. In 2016, his vision for a national grandparenting ministry brought together a gifted team of family, children, and youth ministry leaders to launch this movement of God. His 40 years plus of ministry leadership, including experience as youth pastor, missionary, training staff, international director, and senior executive for Awana, have prepared him for this significant new calling.

Larry has authored books on children's and family ministry and is in high demand as a regular main stage speaker and workshop presenter at conferences. His most recent book, *Overcoming Grandparenting Barriers*, helps grandparents navigate family relationships when things aren't perfect.

In 2012, he was recognized for his lifetime of contribution to Children's Ministry in America by the International Network of Children's Ministry, with their national Legacy Award. Larry and his wife, Diane, live in Riverside, California. They have two children and seven grandchildren.

**Rich Griffith,** D.Min., has over 40 years of ministry experience (30 in youth ministry and 10 as a lead pastor). Rich has been teaching at Toccoa Falls College since 2016 as the associate professor of Youth and Multi-Generational Ministry. Both his Master of Theology and Doctorate (youth, family, and culture) are from Fuller Theological Seminary. Rich completed a second M.A. in organizational leadership from Toccoa Falls College. Rich developed the Youth and Family Doctor of Ministry program for South College and serves on the board of the Association of Youth Ministry Educators.

Rich is a frequent speaker for the D6 Conference, LIFE, NEXT, Intergenerate, and other ministry and leadership conferences. He is a published author in a variety of Zondervan and Youth Specialties materials, and a writer for RootedMinistry.com. He is the author of, *Voices: Helping Our Children and Youth Listen to Wise Counsel* (2023), which was featured on Focus on the Family. He also wrote *Discipleship Is Leadership* (2024), both books are published by D6 Family Ministry. Dr. Griffith is also a part-time pastor at a local church. His most important ministry is to his three sons. He has a special interest in working with churches and families to equip every generation to disciple each other into becoming life-long disciples of Jesus who make more disciples.

**JJ Jones,** D.Min., is closing in on 40 years of ministry experience youth ministry, family ministry, and discipleship (30 plus in youth and family ministry and seven in discipleship). He is an adjunct professor in the Ministry Leadership Department at Toccoa Falls College where he has taught youth ministry, leadership, and spiritual formation classes for eight years. He holds an undergraduate degree in Religion from Union University, a Master of Divinity from Mid-America Baptist Theological Seminary, and a Doctor of Ministry in youth, family, and culture from Fuller Theological Seminary.

JJ is also the pastor of groups at Fellowship Bible Church, a multisite church in the greater Nashville area, where he leads a team overseeing adult ministries. He has a heart for the nation of India, and has led pastor's conferences, marriage conferences with his wife Anna, and has taught at local Bible colleges and seminaries in that country. He and Anna still mentor young couples and families and have a desire to see legacies of generational discipleship beginning with their two grown children and grandchildren.

Dr. Jones has spoken over the years at youth camps and retreats, local parent and marriage conferences, and now nationally at the D6 Conference and on the *D6 Family Ministry Podcast*. He has served on writing teams for Fellowship Resources. This is JJ's first book.

**Kevin M. Jones,** Ed.D., joined the faculty at Cedarville University in 2020. He is a native of Louisville, Kentucky, and has varied experience in public school systems, homeschooling, collegiate level teaching, and administration. He previously held posts at Boyce College and Kentucky State University. He has served as a lay pastor at Buck Run Baptist Church, Forest Baptist Church, and Watson Memorial Baptist Church. Jones' longing is to see fathers build resilient sons and to see teachers and leaders influence the lives of students nationally and internationally, teaching and leading unto the glory of God.

Kevin enjoys playing board games with family—wife and high school sweetheart, Demica, and three children: Kennedi, Kevin Jr, and Karsynn.

**Shelly Melia,** Ph.D., serves as the program director for the Master of Arts in Children's Ministry and the Master of Arts in Family Ministry at Dallas Baptist University. Prior to coming to DBU she served for over 25 years in children's and family ministry in Oklahoma, Florida, and Texas. Dr. Melia is also a Licensed Professional Counselor specializing in grief and resilience. She holds an undergraduate degree from Oklahoma Baptist University, two master's degrees from Southwestern Baptist Theological Seminary and a Doctor of Philosophy from B.H. Carroll Theological Institute.

Dr. Melia has spoken at national conferences such as ETCH Family Ministry Conference, D6 Conference, and the Children's Pastor's Conference. In addition, she is a frequent speaker for local churches and state conventions in Oklahoma, Texas, Georgia, Louisiana, and Missouri. Most recently, she contributed a chapter titled "The Role of Faith or Spirituality in a Child's Response to Loss" to the new book, *Bridging Theory and Practice in Children's Spirituality.*